More praise for
NO MORE LETHAL WAITS

"The emergency department is at the epicentre of many parts of the healthcare system. It is a complex environment interacting not only with different parts of the hospital but also with primary care, home care, and long-term care. Understanding how to get an ED functioning well is an integral part of getting the whole system to work well."

–JOSHUA TEPPER, MD, President and CEO, Health Quality Ontario;
Adjunct Scientist, Institute for Clinical Evaluative Sciences; former
Assistant Deputy Minister of Health, Ontario

"Dr. Whatley's ideas and syntheses of ideas do more for improving the efficiency, effectiveness, safety, timeliness, and equity of urgent care than anything I have seen in writing before. The hard work is now ahead of us to convert these ideas into standard practice."

–DARREN LARSEN, MD, Chief Medical Information Officer, OntarioMD;
Vice Chair, Cancer Quality Council of Ontario

"For the courageous, this book promises to spark discussion; it is a must read for everyone involved in emergency care."

–CHRIS SIMPSON, MD, Chair, Wait Time Alliance,
2014–2015 President, Canadian Medical Association

"This book has been a long time coming. Dr. Whatley demonstrates deep expertise in the effective application of fundamental industrial engineering techniques. While this is not his background and training, the results speak for themselves. Applying these concepts can be a game changer for patient flow."

–JASON GROTO, President of AnalysisWorks,
specializing in patient-flow solutions

"Where's the beef in this book? It's in the sacred cows of emergency medicine that Dr. Whatley kills: waiting rooms, triage, nursing ratios, and more. A must read for anyone frustrated with a system that presumes people must wait."

–JON JOHNSEN, MD, Assistant Professor of Medicine,
Northern Ontario School of Medicine, Thunder Bay

"Addresses in depth the transformation of ED processes necessary to adapt to the current climate of government cost-cutting in healthcare. Having personally experienced many of these changes, I can say that they are neither painless nor perfect for staff or patients but reflect a necessary reality."

–STEPHEN CLUFF, MD, past Medical Director and
Chief of Southlake Emergency Department, Newmarket, Ontario

"Dr. Whatley draws on successful leadership principles from business and industry, empowering conscientious ED and hospital leaders to do is what is right for all patients who come through hospitals' ED gate. A very stimulating and awakening message."

–STEPHEN B. STOKL, MD, Chief of Psychiatry, Southlake Regional Health
Centre; Assistant Professor, Faculty of Medicine, Department of Psychiatry,
University of Toronto; author of *Mentally Speaking*

"*No More Lethal Waits* reads like an ED encounter, moving from main complaint to focused analysis of signs and symptoms to diagnosis and treatment. A to-the-point read for busy leaders who know there's a problem but have not yet seen how to fix it."

–PHIL WHATLEY, MD, Chief of Staff, Riverside Healthcare, Emo, Ontario

"There were multiple times when I laughed followed by an audible 'ahhhhh' in response to one of this book's revolutionary ideas. Dr. Whatley is a true innovator and pioneer in modern medicine."

–JASON PROFETTO, MD, Assistant Clinical Professor, Chair of Clinical Skills,
Undergraduate Medical Program, McMaster University, Hamilton, Ontario

"Some problems seem intractable, only to have someone like Dr. Whatley come along and apply creativity and practicality and suddenly the impossible becomes possible. His advice can be of great benefit to any emergency department tired of the status quo and truly seeking a solution to improve its wait-time performance."

"Candid, clear, inspiring, and practical advice on what really works for excellence in service to our patients. The result is hope. Hope in 10 steps toward a new culture of care."

"Refreshingly frank – a reminder that Emergency failure is really hospital failure. However, improvements to EDs will not be retained until Emergency failure endangers the financial success of hospitals' investments. Hospitals in general must accept some risk and make changes that really work for patients, not just generate committees and more talk."

"With emergency departments desperate to find doctors, we can't find enough spots for all the docs wanting to work in our department at Southlake. The approach described in *No More Lethal Waits* really works for patients and physicians. I have not seen a better way. You won't be disappointed."

Best wishes Shawn

No More Lethal Waits

10 Steps to Transform Canada's Emergency Departments

Shawn Whatley, MD

BPS
books
www.bpsbooks.com

Published in 2016 by
BPS Books
Toronto
www.bpsbooks.com
A division of Bastian Publishing Services Ltd.

ISBN 978-1-77236-031-8 (paperback)
ISBN 978-1-77236-032-5 (ePDF)
ISBN 978-1-77236-032-2 (ePUB)

Cataloguing-in-Publication Data available from Library
and Archives Canada.

Cover and text design: Daniel Crack, Kinetics Design,
www.kdbooks.ca

To everyone who leads emergency care,
especially those without a title

Contents

Preface

PATIENTS do not need to wait for care in emergency departments (EDs). They wait because departments cling to processes and thinking designed to produce waiting. Everyone blames something: overcrowded hospitals, inappropriate visits, older and sicker patients.[1]

Doctors and nurses say, *"Sorry for the wait. It's a really busy day."*

But they aren't surprised when patients fill hallways and loiter around triage without an empty chair or stretcher in sight. Emergency departments have known for decades that they see far more patients at specific times. They also know that the next day after a surge in patient volumes the ED will be backed up with admitted patients waiting to get beds upstairs on the wards. For the most part, really busy days are as predictable as average days.

None of this is news to people working in EDs. Politeness demands apologizing to patients, but the apologies often betray helplessness.

A *New England Journal of Medicine* editorial describes a crowded ED as "more than a nuisance; it is a threat both to individual patients and to overall public health."[2] Inefficient EDs cause more deaths and increased hospital admissions.[3]

Every hour of waiting increases patients' risk of death,[4] adverse events,[5] and preventable errors.[6] Patients suffer longer in pain,[7] get the wrong treatment,[8] and cost more[9] when EDs block up. There is a better way. A proven one. Our team at Southlake Regional Health Centre, Newmarket, Ontario, where, from 2008 to 2014, I was Interim Medical Director of Emergency Services and then Physician Leader of the Emergency Services Program, applied the 10 steps in this book to produce the shortest wait times to see a physician in Ontario. Our team transformed patient flow and wait times by taking, and modifying, successful flow solutions from St. Joseph's Hospital in Toronto. Like that hospital, we became a province-leading performer. There is no reason that our approach can't be used to change emergency care and wait times everywhere.

We learn by association, borrowing the best ideas found around us. This book is no different. It stands on the experience of hundreds of other leaders, providers, patients, and departments. One physician needs special mention, however: Dr. Marko Duic, the man behind the transformation of the ED at St. Joseph's. For 10 years at that hospital, he dreamed up, researched, and refined many of the central ideas discussed in this book. After recruiting him as Chief of the Department of Emergency Medicine (EM) at Southlake, we set to work on improving our processes based on the St. Joseph's experience, while crafting language to flesh out the concepts underlying the processes. We started where St. Joe's left off, and, within two years, Southlake became the top-performing ED in Ontario and sustained its performance as one of the best large departments in Canada in the years that followed. In fact, Southlake continued to innovate flow and actually surpassed the success of St. Joe's. Without Dr. Duic's experience and relentless attack on process, the totality of the advice in this book would not be possible.

Who This Book Is For

This book speaks to leaders: everyone involved with change in emergency departments. Most of the time, responsibility for change falls on the shoulders of senior EM leaders and hospital administrators, people with titles. But, as everyone knows, change never happens without the support of engaged followers who lead from the ground up, as leaders without titles. The word "leaders" throughout this book applies to them, too.

Most leaders have not considered the full approach described here. They may have tried some of the ideas, but not all at once. This book's understanding of flow and efficiency is designed to inspire others with the courage to tackle change. Leaders need confidence to challenge anyone who benefits from making patients wait. Yes, some people would rather see patients languish in waiting rooms than disturb the serenity of the rest of the hospital. Leaders can modify the 10 steps to make them work in their department and in almost any other setting that serves patients with unscheduled visits.

Those of you who are ED leaders, hospital administrators, and system planners often hunger for better ways to organize emergency departments than the standard model. You will find an approach here for becoming less bureaucratic – for leading more and managing less.

This book shows ED leaders how to provide great service, achieve high-quality care, and build a resilient department that can respond to any demand. It shows how to return joy to emergency medicine by doing what is right for patients. The process it describes helps leaders compartmentalize – to abstain from questions of political responsibility and system guilt until patient flow improves. Paradoxically, EDs that separate the issues of flow and politics in this way end up creating EDs that are the stuff of administrators', politicians', and citizens' dreams. Costs per case go down, patient length of stay plummets, and adverse outcomes decrease. *EDs function better when we focus on patients first.*

This book builds on practical patient benefit instead of unthinking adherence to rigid ideas pronounced by administrators and expert consultants. You will need to develop your own opinions about how the content can influence change to your local culture. Together, patient care and patient flow require nuance and grace, not military precision and regularity. As Disraeli put it, "There are so many plans and so many schemes, and so many reasons why there should be neither plans nor schemes."

The ideas in *No More Lethal Waits* work regardless of payment system, politics, and the whims of those who happen to control healthcare. The approach it describes took shape in the publicly funded system of Ontario in which it is against the law to provide medical care for a fee. It will work even better in an open system that allows competition. Nothing needs to stop any emergency department from functioning so patients:

- Never wait in waiting rooms.
- Get seen by a physician in less than an hour.
- Have the shortest possible length of stay.
- Receive the highest-quality care and service.

EDs Need Your Emergency Care

When patients arrive at an ED in acute distress, what happens? Does everyone stop working until more resources arrive, or do they find a way to help, rising to the challenge the best they can?

As emergency personnel, you know that you thrive on managing a crisis. You love it. This book presents the overall dilemma of EDs as an emergency crisis for you to solve, one in dire need of your most creative solutions. EDs cannot turn patients away. They must find ways to see every single patient and do their best. By applying the same attitude you use in saving lives in a crisis, you can create internal solutions for overcrowding and stop waiting for outside help that may never come.

Meaningful improvement requires a paradigm shift in how your team thinks about ED function. Unless you think differently as leaders, not just about patient flow but also about operations, systems, leadership, and incentives, nothing will change. Everything involved in a department needs a second look.

This book addresses obvious cases of silliness that seem impossible to fix.[10] It solves them with common sense and practical wisdom informed by other industries or early clinical practice. This book is not the next fad or utopian design but a call for ED leaders to empower the reason, creativity, and innovation of the professionals working on the front lines of care.

The 10 Steps

The ideas in No More Lethal Waits have been boiled down to 10 steps, each of which is given a chapter in this book:

1 Revamp Triage.

2 Close the Waiting Room.

3 Redefine Nurse-to-Patient Ratios.

4 Use Chairs and Exam Tables, Not Stretchers.

5 Change Scheduling to Meet Patient Needs More Efficiently.

6 Give MDs Responsibility for Flow and Hire Patient Navigators.

7 Use Real-Time Data and Adopt a Full Capacity Protocol.

8 Expect Resistance and Prepare for It.

9 Build on Solid Leadership Principles.

10 Get Political.

The concrete advice sits in the first seven steps, which give all the essentials, the mechanics of change. The last three steps touch on leadership ideas and conceptual problems, which, while further away from practical process change, speak to challenges we struggled through; I believe you will find these three steps useful in sustaining the changes you make through the first seven steps.

This book's approach works best as a total system. Success requires most of the steps to function at the same time. Some of the innovations can be used independently, but most hold together in a synergistic unit. It doesn't work to revamp physician scheduling and do nothing about insufficient nursing staff – likewise closing the waiting room to reduce patient waits while not addressing rigid nurse-to-patient ratios. Success lies in adopting the whole package. Dabbling in the easy parts will improve an ED a bit but make the whole approach look weak. If that is the extent of the challenge in your eyes, you would be better off looking at other approaches that offer small, non-threatening changes.

One thing is for sure: we cannot leave emergency departments untouched and expect the whole healthcare system to improve. However, if we can improve EDs, we can improve the most important element of patient contact with healthcare: the front door of every hospital.

STEP#1

Revamp Triage

PATIENTS go to an emergency department expecting efficient, high-quality care: the right diagnosis, effective treatment, and a great outcome in the shortest possible time. Patients expect triage nurses to assure patient safety by identifying those at risk and moving them rapidly into (scarce) available care spaces.[11] This is an impossible task. While it's easy to sort dying patients, it can be impossible to sort undifferentiated, mid-acuity patients. Before we made changes at Southlake Regional Health Centre, in Newmarket, Ontario, and before our "mentor hospital," St. Joseph's, in Toronto, did so, both hospitals had horror stories about patients crashing in waiting rooms. Patients did not look that sick at triage but still crumpled before getting a bed.

During a brief triage encounter, nurses can miss patients with subdural hemorrhage who just appear to be "drunk," or with necrotizing fasciitis who just have "leg pain."[12]

Patients continue to deteriorate and die in ED waiting rooms despite skilled physicians and nurses doing the best they can.[13]

Patients blocked outside triage, in the waiting room, wait in an area where there is no chance they will receive the care they need. They're not getting a diagnosis, management, or a disposition. Value is not being added, and flow has stopped. Think about it from the patients' point of view. They must wonder about the number of trained nurses deployed at the front door, seemingly protecting the department from patients rather than expediting their access to care. Which brings us to the whole issue of triage.

The Problem with Triage

Devotion to triage tops all other sacred cows in emergency medicine.

Triage is almost synonymous with emergency medicine.[14] Patients endure it, nurses believe it must be done, and physicians expect long nursing notes with vital signs before they see a patient.

Triage serves providers. It fulfills our expectations of what defines a good emergency visit. Triage has become so much a part of emergency medicine that EDs apply a good, thorough triaging on patients even when the ED has open beds inside and nurses and physicians are at the ready.

Why do those who work in EDs have such faith in triage? Think about it. Would you yourself tolerate the same experience at a computer store? Consider the following scenario.

You are frustrated because you earn a living with your computer, and you cannot work on an important project because the machine refuses to boot up. You usually take your computer to a local technician, but his shop closed early, so you lug it in to one of the repair stores you find in the mall.

The store is packed with customer line-ups. The first line leads to a service agent who wants to know if you have any pirated software on your computer. Then he asks a long list of useless questions like, *"Have you travelled near an industrial magnet recently?"* Then he directs you to take a number to see the sorting service assistant.

After over an hour of waiting, you get 20 minutes with the sorting service assistant, who probes your complaint to decide which part of the store to send you to so the service technicians can best address your particular issue.

The probing ends with, "*You know, this sort of problem could easily have been addressed by your local technician. We are very, very busy taking care of major problems. It's always best to check with your local tech before just running to your closest mall shop.*"

From there, you are sent to see the cashier to register your issue in their service computer system. She asks your name – "*Could you please spell that again, slowly?*" – address, phone number, social insurance number, date of birth, date of purchase, recent changes of address, and other questions tangentially related to the issues with your computer. Then, she asks for your credit card number, "*just in case we need to apply any costs not covered by warranty.*"

After this, you are sentenced to sit in an area with 24 hard plastic chairs and told to wait until you hear your name called.

"*Some technical issues require attention before the store closes and take more time to fix, so you will not be called up in the order you arrived,*" the cashier says.

Finally, four hours after you arrived at the mall, you get called to see another service assistant, who begins asking you all the same questions the sorting assistant asked you. The assistant enters all the details on an eight-page form with dozens of tiny boxes and blanks that must be filled (to accurately track issues for future reference).

"*The technicians are very backed up because Monday afternoons are always the busiest day of the week,*" the third service assistant says. "*Tuesday mornings are much better. But, they will try their best to get your concern soon, unless some other more important concern pulls the technician away.*"

Who was being served in this story? What would you think of such an operation?

How We Got Here

As far as we know, Napoleon's surgeon invented triage when he started sorting crowds of mangled soldiers on the battlefield.[15] He wanted to quickly determine which wounded men were most likely to return to battle and care for them first. Military triage got soldiers back into fighting action and left seriously wounded comrades to die.

In the olden days of emergency medicine (30 years ago), physicians usually saw patients soon after registration, or sometimes even before registration. Especially on overnight shifts, patients were brought straight inside emergency departments and were seen by a nurse and physician, often at the same time.

In the 1990s, governments, and, in the United States, Health Maintenance Operations (HMOs), ran short of money. They started to drastically trim hospital budgets and close in-patient beds. They thought all the beds should be full, all the time, to improve efficiency. Businesses that strive to keep customer service people maximally busy, all the time, do so only by making customers wait in lines. The lines might be shorter at times, but there must always be a line.

In the case of hospitals, patients waiting for beds on the in-patient wards started to line up in emergency departments. ED stretchers became the favourite spot to park admitted patients while in-patient wards stayed "full." ("Full" is defined by the number of staff working on the wards, not by the number of beds.)

Historically, emergency providers always saw patients on stretchers. During the busiest hours of the day, patients often had just a short wait before they were seen. But as more and more stretchers filled with admitted patients, EDs started leaving patients in the waiting room longer.

Eventually, waiting rooms became full, all the time, as patients waited to get inside to be seen on a stretcher. Departments assigned nurses to spend more time trying to figure out whether a patient's complaint merited a short, or long, wait to be seen. Triage turned into primary care nursing for new arrivals and the crowd of patients warehoused in the waiting room.

The Canadian Association of Emergency Physicians states:

Triage in the simplest term [sic] is the sorting or prioritizing of items (clients, patients, tasks...). Some form of triaging has been in place, formally or informally since the first ED opened...Efficient management of an ED requires a team of providers capable of correctly identifying patients' needs, setting priorities and implementing appropriate treatment, investigation and disposition.[16]

At its simplest, triage is sorting and prioritizing patients.[17] Long before triage nurses existed, registration clerks sent patients in to the ED who looked too sick to register. Informal triage of some sort has existed since the first ED opened. An ED without any triage would be like a snowman without snow.[18]

Formal triage, triage training, and the "triage nurse" are more recent developments. The triage role has expanded far beyond the simple description above.

Modern triage nurses still collect a presenting complaint, determine acuity, and determine the best care location. But in many EDs, triage involves nurses and other personnel in taking a history, performing a limited physical exam, gathering past medical history, screening for influenza-like illness and domestic violence, asking why patients did not try going to their family physician or local clinic, recording a list of medications and allergies, performing vital signs, advising patients what to expect during their ED stay, "educating" patients about better places they could have gone for care, reassessing patients in the waiting room, and answering questions about parking, bathrooms, and cafeteria hours.

In fact, busy EDs now have up to four triage nurses involved in the assessment, reassessment, and education of patients waiting in waiting rooms. Some departments even add pre-triage screeners to sort the crowd waiting for triage before the actual waiting begins.[19]

In most settings, triage is a barrier between the hordes waiting outside and the lucky few called inside for care.

From Triage to Value, Flow, Efficiency, and Quality

Again, patients expect the right diagnosis, effective treatment, and a great outcome in the shortest possible time. Emergency providers want the same.

But many departments struggle with this. They don't have enough resources, and they use the resources they have poorly. Instead of meeting patient expectations as efficiently as possible, they make patients wait in one line-up after another, undergo redundant processes, and endure rituals (of questionable benefit) they don't understand.

If we hope to meet patient expectations without useless process, we need language to describe it. The language of optimal process consists of four terms: value, flow, efficiency, and quality.

Value is whatever benefits patients,[20] what an informed patient would be willing to pay for. When an emergency nurse wants a medical opinion about her red eye, she turns to a physician and asks. If she found value in standing in line, getting triaged and registered, waiting for a secondary nursing assessment, and finally getting seen by an emergency physician, she would do it. But she knows what adds value: a diagnosis and treatment plan.

Flow is the continuous addition of value as patients journey through the system. Patients often need more than just a physical examination to get a diagnosis. Tests, treatments, and re-examination use up patients' time. If patients always get something done with no waiting (something that informed customers would pay for), we can say flow exists. Flow stops when delays happen between tests, treatment, and examination.[21]

Efficiency is maximizing value-added with the resources available.[22] Very efficient departments squeeze the most value out of available resources. Inefficiency occurs when EDs use resources – staff time, supplies, and facilities – for things that do not add value.

Quality often gets defined as safe, effective, patient-centred, timely, efficient, and equitable care.[23] As we will discuss later, timely care can literally make the difference between life and death in emergency departments. For EDs, time equals quality for many things. We will return to this below.

For now, let's drill down on value, flow, efficiency, and quality.

What Is Value?

Over time, ED processes have become more and more complicated. From a patient and outcome perspective, much of the standard ED process adds little or no value.

If value is what an informed patient would be willing to pay for, does that make value nothing more than patients' wants? In healthcare, anything that provides health benefit is value-added. This opens debate on how to define "health" and "benefit." Does health include psychological health? Does benefit include happiness? This could turn into a discussion, like President Clinton's, about what the meaning of "is" is.

In emergency medicine, the definition of "health" usually gets pared down far more than it might in a private office. Emergency providers tend to focus quickly on physical issues and pay only superficial attention to psychosocial issues. Of course, this can get us into trouble; often the physical issue is buried in the psychosocial. Regardless, emergency providers tend to lean heavily on providing a technological product for physical problems, with as pleasant a patient experience as possible.

Value adds health benefit for patients.

What Is Flow?

So, how does value relate to flow? We all know when flow is absent. Patients sit, charts pile up, families fidget, no one moves; stasis prevails. Flow implies movement, velocity, and action.

Moving patients around from one spot in the ED to another can give the impression of flow. Popular theme parks like Disney have mastered the psychology of waiting. They use distractions to keep people from growing restless as they wait for a ride.

But more than just movement, flow is the continuous addition of value as patients move through the system. In fact, the best flow often happens when there appears to be very little movement, when the department looks calm. We can say, if every patient is getting an assessment, investigation, or treatment performed, that flow is excellent even without physical movement.

Mayer and Jensen propose that "flow exists to the extent that value is added to a product or service during a patient's journey through the queues and service transitions in healthcare. In other words, at each step of the patient's journey, those providing care should ask the following: Does this add value? How does this add value?"[24]

Flow Inhibitors

Most often, we ED providers – doctors, nurses, and allied staff – stop flow. We make patients wait while we do other things. Whether we batch, do things inefficiently, or just get overwhelmed with the amount of work necessary, we stop flow. We make it look like delays are the fault of slow lab turnarounds or a shortage of supplies, but most often the problem is that we choose to work in ways that decrease flow.

Sometimes, we decrease flow because we think it will create less work for us. *If I go slow with my patients, someone else will pick up the slack.* This leads to a critical axiom that relates flow and workload: *decreased flow* ⇨ *increased length of stay* ⇨ *increased workload.*

Revamp Triage

Taking our time, working slowly, and doing "a really good job" decreases patient flow and increases patient length of stay. Every hour a patient spends in the ED requires nursing care. Notwithstanding what I just said about working slowly, flow does not mean providing faster, inadequate care, or cutting corners with patients. Depending on *why* we're spending a bit longer time with patients, this kind of slowing down can add value that will save time later. Indeed, retaining time-consuming, high-value activities and eliminating low-value activities is likely to provide all patients a shorter and more efficient journey.

Non-value-added patient waiting does not improve health outcomes in emergency medicine. This is seen most often when patients wait for a test, a provider, or an in-patient bed, but flow also stops during many time-honoured emergency processes.

The best way to decrease workload is to work hard to increase patient flow.

Focus on Adjusting Flow, Not Capacity

Patient volumes and arrivals need to match flow, not physical capacity. Simply adding millions of dollars of extra physical capacity will not guarantee better flow for patients.[25] Sure, EDs always need more beds, but they need increased flow *more*. Flow doesn't just mean flow *out of* the hospital, which is the obsession of cash-strapped hospital administrators. Patient flow means flow *in to* a hospital, too.

We often blame long-term care or families for not taking patients home, as though there would be no waiting if no alternate level of care patients (ALC, patients who need long-term care) came to the hospital.[26] Or we blame the in-patient wards for not taking patients out of our EDs sooner. We did not have an ALC problem years ago, but we still had admitted patients in the ED. ALC is a factor impeding flow, but it's not the only one.

Until we develop a culture of getting every patient inside

– getting them in to the ED and up to the wards – when they present, and not just when we are ready for them, we will never get rid of patient waiting or be truly efficient.

What Is Efficiency?

Operational efficiency relates to how well the whole department works, how far EDs stretch resources. Efficiency is defined by the ratio of value-added to the cost of providing it, with people, infrastructure, technology, and drugs: *efficiency = value / cost.*

Efficiency means achieving maximum patient benefit with the resources available. EDs waste resources if activities do not add value, stealing potential health benefit (value) from other patients in need.

Efficiency and flow improve when we minimize waiting and other non-value-added activities.

What Is Quality?

No one has a great definition of quality for all care in every possible clinical setting. We know it when it's present, but we cannot describe it precisely across healthcare.

In emergency medicine in Canada, a guide to understanding quality comes from the Institute for Clinical Evaluative Sciences (ICES) *Consensus on Evidence-Based Quality of Care Indicators for Canadian Emergency Departments, 2010.*[27] As far as evidence-based literature goes, it gives a picture of what quality means in emergency care.

The ICES scientists narrowed down 48 indicators of quality from peer-reviewed studies. Of the 48, 23 are related to time in one way or another, and 16 depend entirely on time. For example:

- Time to antibiotics.
- Time to consultation.
- Time to first physician assessment.

In emergency medicine, for most of the care and service provided, *time = quality*. Unlike many other specialties, where observation and delay can be helpful, in emergency medicine a difference of minutes can save lives. ED waits cause suffering and death.[28] No doubt, quality also includes providing the right treatment for the right problem. It involves consistency, great communication, discharge excellence, and appropriate follow-up. Quality requires peak team performance, prompt reassessments, and high-functioning laboratory and diagnostic imaging services. All these things are necessary for high-quality EM care.

But no matter how great the product is when it finally gets to the patient, it is low-quality care if it is not delivered in a timely fashion. You can have great physicians and nurses, with all the right resources, but if you make patients wait, you are not delivering high-quality care. This concept is so critical, it begs to be pounded one more time.

Is Your ED High in Quality?

Your department delivers second-rate emergency medical care if you make patients wait.

Missed diagnoses, errors of judgment, and clinical mistakes can be hard to spot. Since time to treatment equals quality for much of emergency medicine, it is the easiest way to quickly assess emergency department quality.

Does your ED have:

1 *A long line at triage?* The most at-risk patients stand in line waiting for triage. Patients walk in with a potentially lethal problem every shift. Until they have been seen, they are unsafe. Line-ups at triage signal low quality.

2 *A long triage process?* Triage should be sorting, not a primary nursing assessment. Patients need a diagnosis and treatment. How much extra work do the triage nurses perform that

could be done elsewhere? A long triage process causes delay and low-quality care.

3 *Registration delay?* Collecting demographics to make a chart does not add value for patients; it only delays life-saving care. We need the information, but it must be to the point.

4 *A packed waiting room?* Patients never need to wait in the waiting room. Besides lowering quality, patients hate waiting rooms. They are dirty, unpleasant, and unsafe.

5 *Patients repeating their story over and over?* Providers should quickly check what others have recorded, verify the facts, and ask additional questions. A system in which each provider starts the process all over again drives patients nuts, decreases efficiency, and causes delay.

In general, second-rate EDs put provider interests before patient interests. To add insult to (untreated) injury, privileged patients never experience delays like the *hoi polloi.* Doctors and nurses working in the department get immediate access when they have medical concerns. For example, a nurse with chest pain gets her colleague to do an ECG and takes it immediately to the physician on duty. If the ECG raises concern, the nurse chews some ASA and has her colleague draw cardiac blood-work, while the triage nurse and registration clerk quickly make a chart.

Privileged patients get what they need, first. Paperwork, policy, and process come second. Meanwhile, on the *standard model*, everyone else waits to have their medical needs met until we, the providers, have our screening-triaging-charting-registering-workflow needs met.

Triage In, *Not* Out

We must revisit triage now, in light of the discussion above about changing our language to value, flow, efficiency, and quality. There must be triage, but if it does not consist of rapid sorting, it is not triage at all.

As mentioned, modern triage redefined the term "triage" to include long interviews, multiple forms, medication reconciliation, past medical history, allergy lists, infection control screening, extensive sets of vital signs, patient examination, patient education, wound inspection, and answering patients' questions about waits, parking, directions, and vending machine locations...

Maybe that's a good thing? Maybe patients want to come to the ED to get a really thorough triage?

No, patients come to the ED to get a diagnosis and treatment. Diagnostic and treatment delay subtracts value and increases the risk of harm to patients.

Triage must add value by getting patients to the care they need, as quickly as possible. We must attack anything that stands in the way of patient care. Quality care depends on timely assessment and treatment. Triage adds value only if it facilitates timely care. Triage should never bottleneck flow; there should never be a line-up to see the triage nurse.

If we are serious about improving patient flow, we must unload all the duties we've piled onto triage. In fact, if hospitals insist on running waiting rooms like clinical areas, patients would be better served if we assigned nurses to care for the patients in the waiting room like a separate ward instead of shackling triage nurses with non-value-added work pretending it makes things safer.

Triage – historical triage – should still be the first step patients experience after entering the ED. In a minute or two, skilled nurses can determine presenting complaint and CTAS (Canadian Triage and Acuity Score) and send patients to the best care location. Patients in a care area, even if less than ideal, get care faster than those the triage nurse sends to the waiting room. The waiting room is never the best or safest place to put patients.

Care occurs inside the department, not at triage, so why not move the nurses and patients inside? We did this. We found that reducing triage complexity, and removing patients from the waiting room, greatly reduces the delay and cost of triage. We shortened triage to five minutes per patient. Nurses were able to process 10 to 12 patients per hour with minimal waiting. Using one nurse at triage instead of three meant the other two nurses could be redeployed to care for patients inside. They could cover up to 12 more stretchers or care spaces. Based on an average patient length of stay of four hours, 70 more patients per day could receive necessary care than if the same two nurses spent their day in triage.

Patients will still wait when they are brought straight inside, but they will wait less. And they wait in areas where they can get the care they need. Bringing patients straight inside works best when it is the only place they can go. Which brings us to step #2: you have to close your waiting room.

REVAMP TRIAGE

STEP# *2*

Close the Waiting Room

IMPROVING efficiency at triage (step #1) will not improve flow if we insist on making patients wait in the waiting room. Our team used LEAN management thinking to run a number of events to make triage faster, and they all helped. But when the ED became "full," patients waited just as long as they always did – they just spent less time with the triage nurse! Efficient triage is not enough.

Close Waiting Room Reservoirs

Triage is an obstruction that makes the waiting room a reservoir. The waiting room bunches patients until triage or managers let patients get the care they need. Patients do not come to the ED to get stopped in the waiting room. They want to keep moving as quickly as possible. No matter how great, entertaining, clean, or comfortable they may be, waiting rooms do not benefit patients.

The sad fact is that hospitals create waiting rooms to make work easier for doctors and nurses. Waiting rooms help providers, not patients. They decrease the chaos of provider work environments but do nothing to fix the chaos and panic patients feel as they wait to get seen. Why do you think hospitals usually build security offices next to ED waiting rooms? Because that's where security is likely to be needed most, to quell an uprising of waiting patients.

At St. Joseph's in Toronto and Southlake in Newmarket, patients are brought directly in to the department after a quick screening triage. This allows providers to see, feel, and respond to swells in patient volume. The instant feedback on patient demand transforms provider behaviour, improves wait times, and increases quality.

Perhaps the biggest secret to improved ED function is to stop triaging patients out to the waiting room. Don't let triage be an obstruction. Bring patients straight in to see care providers.

Increased Capacity Is Not the Answer

Instead of building resilience and maximizing flow, most departments find it easier to build extra capacity. New capacity takes centre stage in photos and prominent mention in ad covers. Hospital tours always include shiny new clinical space. But there's actually a risk to new clinical capacity, the risk of adding little or no value for patients.[29] New capacity often becomes a reservoir that slows patient flow. New capacity – patient wards, waiting rooms, bigger clinics, bigger emergency departments – can ruin patient flow, if we let it.

Wait times lengthen with increased capacity unless pressure increases to overcome the decreased flow caused by the increased capacity. New in-patient wards decrease flow – the exact opposite of what we hoped for – unless an increase in pressure on flow offsets the drop in flow caused by new capacity.

Reservoirs in Healthcare

Picture a violent river pouring through a narrow canyon. It looks completely unmanageable until it reaches a giant dam, which creates a reservoir where the river slows to a standstill. Reservoirs in healthcare convert high-flow, hard-to-manage situations into low-flow, contained events. They allow providers to meter out patients instead of having to see them all at once. Triage trickles patients into the ED from the waiting room. In-patient wards trickle patients on to in-patient beds, when nurses and doctors are ready to see them. Reservoirs are familiar and socially acceptable, a common solution to high-flow demands. In fact, most institutions actually pride themselves on the size of their reservoirs. In the context of EDs, reservoirs decrease chaos and make *providers* feel safe. And the patients? They feel just as scared and unsafe waiting in a reservoir as they did when they arrived at the department.

Bottlenecks and Flow Stoppers

But dams have a legitimacy – providing electric power – that triage systems do not have. "Bottleneck" is a better metaphor for what happens in EDs. The term became part everyday conversation after Eli Goldratt popularized it in his book *The Goal*, an interesting fable based on the otherwise dry theory of constraints.[30] *The Goal* has been a business classic for over two decades, spawning a pile of other great narrative business books. It tells the story of a factory that had to improve or face closure. It shows the senior executive trying to improve efficiency, fast, such as by reducing inventory and batching. But success comes only when he understands bottlenecks and how to deal with them.

A bottleneck limits the speed of an entire production. It has a maximum speed, and every other process must wait for it. Bottlenecks are built into healthcare processes everywhere. For example, triage is a classic bottleneck. Everyone goes through triage, and triage has a maximum speed based on triage protocols and standards. Bottlenecks are a common experience in the world of the ED. They must be identified and tackled to improve flow. Bottlenecks need to be:

1 Unblocked, by giving work to some other process.

2 Removed, by eliminating a process completely.

3 Improved, by removing wasteful steps in processes to increase speed.

4 Put in parallel.

Nearly every step in a patient's journey can stop flow. Even the most LEANed process requires fanatical vigilance to guarantee patients don't get stopped as they move through our hospitals.

In industry, bottlenecks turn up as critical processing steps whose maximum speed determines the maximum speed of a whole production line. In emergency medicine, *bottlenecks change all the time.* They wreak havoc by showing up unexpectedly. In fact, a dozen different things could be a bottleneck – the rate-limiting step – over one day in the ED: in the morning, nurse shortages from sick calls; in the afternoon, lack of beds; at night, lack of hospital support staff. Most folks in EDs have a favourite bottleneck they like to blame:

- *"If only we had more beds. If only we didn't have admitted patients!"*
- *"If only we didn't have such slow docs!"*
- *"If only we had more (or faster) nurses!"*
- *"If only we had more space!"*

It seems we pick one bottleneck – something usually out of our control – as a way to remove responsibility for addressing the bottlenecks that are in our control.

There's only one way to guarantee that a bottleneck will never slow patient flow in your ED, and that is parallel processing. Even if you improve a bottleneck in other ways, it can still cause delays in sequential processes. Putting a bottleneck in parallel with other processes is the key to even better improvements.

Parallel Processing

Like one boxcar following another in a train, some things in EDs need to be processed sequentially, e.g., sutures before dressing. But in other parts of ED work, e.g., secondary nursing assessments, lab work, registration, and dozens more, insisting on doing things in order creates bottlenecks. Parallel processing unhitches the boxcars and lets them all run on separate tracks at the same time. That way, if any process stops, all the others can continue.

Closing the waiting room requires parallel processing. I realize this may sound threatening to many ED leaders and workers. Medicine loves process and sequence. Many of the sacred cows in emergency medicine are core to sequential processing:

1 Triage followed by

2 Secondary Assessment followed by

3 MD assessments followed by

4 Lab and DI followed by

5 Portering...

6 Reassessments...

7 Discharge

Most providers fight to keep care in sequence. It's what we're used to. We were trained to think that these steps must occur in sequence, with no step beginning until the previous step is complete. But sequential processing creates bottlenecks: queues of patients waiting for care. In some hospitals, for example, registration clerks sit beside triage RNs. Triage and registration occur at the same time; they happen in parallel. Parallel processing works all over the ED to virtually eliminate the impact of bottlenecks, greatly improving overall efficiency.

Of all medical people, we emergency providers should not

feel threatened by parallel processing. Do we not often ignore sequential process for our sickest patients? We whisk acutely ill patients into a resuscitation room where every process happens at once: lab draws, portable x-rays, intubation, registration, RN assessment, MD assessment, charting, vitals, medical history... Everything happens at the same time, in parallel. In these cases, nothing comes between patients and the care they need, in the shortest time possible.

When we need to be our best for our sickest patients, we go parallel. Why not do it all the time?

Unless it is critical to patient care, efficient ED teams eliminate sequential processes at every opportunity. Rearrange your inflow processes as follows:

1　Historical triage (quick sorting).

2　Everything else.

Once patients have been triaged into the ED, care should unfold in parallel. If a nurse is busy, patients can see a doctor first. If no doctor is available, nurses can initiate medical directives – but not by reflex with every patient. And registration can happen anytime.

Make Exceptions for Everyone

None of this is new to emergency medicine. We just don't apply it consistently. Putting patients' needs first happens all the time, for our sickest patients and when we choose to broaden our definition of acuity:

- As mentioned above, colleagues in the ED get seen without any waiting (triage, registration, waiting room, etc.).
- Local dignitaries – politicians, sports stars, and actors – never get stuck in waiting rooms for hours. (*"It would be too distracting for the other patients."*)
- Friends and family of ED staff get straight in to see physicians.

In contrast to the way surgery units handle wait lists, creating rigid and explicit queues, EDs process patients with a great deal of latitude. Everything from patient anxiety, demeanour, and civility can impact how quickly patients are seen. So it's no surprise that doctors and nurses can use a "get seen right away even if there's no chair to sit in" approach for privileged patients. We get away with it because sorting and triage are vague; it's not as obvious to patients that other patients are being whisked through the system as it would be if everyone was in a queue for operating room spots.

However, if we adjust process some of the time, why not do so all the time for everyone?

Do Everything at the Same Time

After an initial critical look by an experienced nurse, done at the moment of the patient's initial arrival, everything else involved in an ED visit can be done in parallel. Nothing in law or in practice says a chart has to be made first, or a full triage assessment has to be done first. Everything else should get done "as soon as possible." Whoever can get to the patient first should get started on their part of the process, even if it means they cannot complete it before another provider arrives.

In EDs that truly adopt this thinking, MDs may assess and discharge a patient before the patient even sees an RN. Or Lab/DI and discharge planning may get involved before an MD gets to a patient. This requires huge flexibility for providers bound by historical processes. Sequential steps should not be tolerated as an excuse for making patients wait.

Objections

These ideas always raise objections about (1) volumes, (2) appropriateness of care, (3) costs, and (4) efficiency. We'll deal with these in the next step in the context of nurses and patients. For now, let's look at them primarily from the point of view of hospital administrators and system planners.

1 Won't It Increase Volume?

Hospital administrators see volume as increased cost. System planners worry about the inefficiency of ED care compared with other options. Administrators tend to worry about increased patient volumes driving up costs and destroying efficiency. Once a community learns that their emergency department has no waiting room and very short wait times to see a physician, low-acuity patients might overwhelm the ED and crush efficiency. Won't surging lines of patients destroy budgets and burn out staff? Shouldn't EDs focus only on *real* emergencies?

High Acuity vs. High Volume

Sometimes common knowledge is neither common nor knowledge, including the dream of a high-acuity-only ED. We often hear: *"If the ED only saw 'true emergencies,' ED crowding and costs would improve."* And, *"Many patients don't need to be in the ED. We would save money by sending them somewhere else."*

The dream of high-acuity, "true-emergency" EDs assumes a number of things, including:

- It's possible to educate patients to go elsewhere.
- Patients have somewhere else to get care.
- Staff can safely tell who is a "true emergency" and can send all others elsewhere.
- Low-acuity patients crowd the ED and shouldn't be there.
- We can save money by decreasing low-acuity ED visits.

This is nonsense. Patients attend the ED for access, not because they are stupid. Most patients don't need education. Patients come to harm if sent elsewhere. According to The Canadian Association of Emergency Physicians statement on overcrowding, low-acuity patients do *not* crowd the ED; they cycle through quickly.[31] It's sick, admitted patients who crowd the ED. And marginal costs for minor patient complaints are minuscule – pennies compared with the cost of keeping the ED open.

Clusters of Emergencies, Idleness in Between

Furthermore, "true emergencies" don't trickle in one at a time. They often show up in batches. Leaders should ask:

Has our ED ever had two resuscitations at the same time?
How about three?
Even four?

These scenarios are *not* rare. In larger EDs, three critically ill patients commonly present at the same time. Most of us can recall a time when four such patients showed up within minutes. Each critically ill patient requires up to four nurses, a physician, a respiratory technician, and more. Guaranteeing immediate care may demand up to 16 nurses, a team of allied health providers, and a group of MDs in the department ready to work 24/7.

What would you have your nurses, physicians, and techs do between treating "true emergencies"? Idleness equals waste; it kills efficiency. But communities need emergency resources capable of covering anything that might happen. Small EDs often have many hours when they see very few patients. An acute care resource running at anything less than full capacity wastes money.

Has anyone solved this in healthcare? Aside from closing EDs, how can we improve efficiency for resources designed to handle surges of acute need?

Fire departments face the same problem. Fire crews spend most of their time getting ready to work. Their full emergency capacity is rarely used. Most of their time is spent on standby. Many US fire departments use firemen as first responders to decrease the inefficiency of idle emergency services.

Hospitals do something similar with their trauma rooms. Larger hospitals keep one or more operating rooms open and staffed, at great cost, in case trauma or emergency surgeries come in. Idle trauma rooms cost a ton of money. Hospitals often recover some of the costs by managing non-emergency cases, especially if the team has already been called in.

Hospitals eliminate idleness to increase efficiency. Hospitals *recover cost and gain efficiency by using the trauma room for less urgent, non-trauma patients!*

Even *if* there was a way to figure out which patients were "true emergencies," EDs large enough to manage all such emergencies in a community would stand idle much of the time at *huge* cost. *EDs recover cost and gain efficiency by seeing less-acute patients just like trauma rooms gain efficiency by being used for elective surgery while on standby.*

The efficiency found in an ED that never sits idle will always crush a mythical high-acuity ED. The trouble is, some staff like to have a little waste in the system. (This is tackled in the next step.)

Considering it another way, a worry about increased volumes seems a terrible reason to not improve service. If volumes increase because your service is great, so be it. Hopefully, other EDs in the area will improve, too. Medicare rations care by making patients wait in lines, so system planners naturally wring their hands when waits are removed and providers talk about abundance. (More on abundance later.) If planners want patients to seek care elsewhere, they need to design the system to incentivize patients to do so.

2 Appropriateness of Care: Can't Most Patients Be Seen in a Clinic?

This question relates to the high-acuity efficiency discussion above, but it adds another factor that administrators and system planners raise, often following the lead of ED doctors, nurses, and leaders themselves. Nothing costs as much as care provided in the emergency department, goes the argument; therefore, appropriate patients should be sent straight to a clinic where they will be seen immediately. A clinic could assess patients, perform routine investigations, get urgent access to x-rays, and even provide IV treatment.

And how would these costs differ from ED care?

Fixed costs for EDs are huge, but it costs EDs very little to see more low-acuity patients – far less than the cost of building a separate clinic. And, low-acuity patients *never* block up the ED.

Furthermore, suggesting that patients could be seen elsewhere paints them as undeserving of emergency care; it assumes that patients can be accurately sorted and sent to a clinic.

No method can guarantee that patients sent away from an ED won't come to harm. All EM staff have seen patients triaged to a minor treatment area only to be admitted to the ICU or sent for emergency surgery.[32] Sore throats or back pain can turn out to be life-threatening cases of epiglottitis or aortic dissection. Why not see them in the ED?

3 What About Increased Costs?

Hospital administrators lose more sleep thinking about two financial issues – money and efficiency – than they do over patient complaints and labour strife.

In Canada, most hospitals still use a global budget for most spending. They receive funds each year to care for the patients in their catchment area. Canada is the last country in the world to rely so heavily on this approach, and attempts have been made to change it.

In the past, administrators didn't have to worry about efficiency. Their focus was on staying within budget, which they did by cutting spending on care. Cutting service saves money. The easiest way to cut service is to lay off staff. For example, cutting one nursing position saves approximately $500,000 (it takes 4.5 nurses to cover one position). But nurses are well protected by their union. So, administrators often eye other staff positions to eliminate completely. It feels safer killing off a whole species of providers, such as cast technicians, than taking out just a few of a larger group. By eliminating a particular type of position, no comrades are left behind to foment discord.

But I digress. Cutting service to stay within budget makes the bottom line look great on a balance sheet. However, cuts and savings give administrators only a moment of glory with hospital boards these days. Country club boards that rubber-stamped financial reports have disappeared. Board members have greater financial experience today; they know a wasteful, inefficient department does not warrant praise just for staying within budget. Financially literate board members look for something more: cost per case.

4 Shouldn't We Concentrate on Efficiency?

Emergency departments that drive down their cost per case create an unarguable case for more financial support from the hospital. Ultra-efficient EDs become the darling of hospital boards. On top of that, savvy boards love EDs that show growth in patient volumes coupled with a decrease in cost per patient visit. Hospital boards take pride knowing their ED serves more patients than other EDs nearby. In the schoolyard of hospital leadership, a huge operating budget warrants a certain swagger, but only if costs per case stay low. Great organizations run efficiently and provide service for much less than competitors. Giant budgets that waste money embarrass boards with very high costs per patient. Nothing solidifies bragging rights about a large budget than being able to follow up with, *"And we run the most efficient hospital in the province on a cost-per-case basis."*

Rocks in a Bucket

Rocks in a bucket make for a good analogy to explain hospital efficiency and cost per case. Imagine the total care capacity of a hospital as a giant bucket. The volume of the bucket represents the amount of work a hospital can do: the total amount of hours of human resources, raw materials, supplies, facility expenses (heat, hydro), and everything else the hospital has to use for patient services.

Now imagine that the rocks represent patients, or discrete chunks of care. You need to fill the bucket with rocks (i.e., patients). Some patients use up huge amounts of hospital resources. Others use very little. Hospitals have to serve both kinds of patients, but especially the sickest patients, or biggest rocks.

To maximize hospital efficiency, we must figure out how to get the most rocks into our bucket with as little air space, or waste, as possible, using all sizes of rocks. How can we maximize the density, the mass of rock per unit of bucket volume, of our bucket? Or in other words, how can we maximize the efficiency, the amount of service per dollar of capacity, in our hospitals?

Of course, buckets packed with the smallest rocks end up most fully packed. Unfortunately, hospitals cannot serve only the easiest patients, the smallest rocks.

Children who work on filling buckets as an exercise realize they have to get the big rocks into a bucket first. Putting in the smallest rocks first leaves no room for the big ones. And putting only big rocks into a bucket leaves way too much wasted space where small rocks could fit. But big rocks interspersed with plenty of small rocks guarantees that every bit of space gets filled.

People confuse the total capacity of care – the volume of the bucket – with the total cost of the capacity of care. While related, they are two separate things. The bucket's volume represents chunks of care, discrete variables. Compared with the cost of discrete chunks of care, funding represents a continuous variable. It can be chopped up, down to the penny. EDs can boost efficiency by using the capacity required to care for the sickest patients to provide for lower-acuity patients between arrivals of sick patients.

A critical point hides in this discussion about efficiency. An ED that uses all its budget on the sickest patients, all the time, has zero capacity left to respond to extra patient demand. Such an ED has zero resilience and presents a major risk to patient safety. If hospitals want high-quality care, and to protect their staff from burnout, they need to build resilience and stop grasping at a utopian dream of a high-acuity-only ED. This leads us to the next step, redefining nurse-to-patient ratios.

STEP# 3

Redefine Nurse-to-Patient Ratios

THE first two steps – doing triage faster (triaging in rather than out) and closing the waiting room – may have you thinking, "Bringing all the patients inside sounds great, but who's going to take care of them?" This question raises the issue of nurse-to-patient ratios.

In most EDs, patients don't "count" until they make it to a care space in the department. Once patients are inside, most EDs adhere rigidly to a 4:1 nursing ratio even though there might be 60 patients in the waiting room managed by 3 triage nurses, a 20:1 ratio.

Emergency providers inside the ED work as though they are not responsible for the crowds in the waiting room. We put our heads down and focus on the one patient in front of us. We provide, or aim for, what we believe to be "perfect" care for the few patients allowed in. This approach preserves many non-value-added conventions. Instead, we need emergency teams to start considering *all* the patients in the department at any given moment.

If 12 nurses are on shift and 120 patients are registered in the ED, the overall nursing ratio for the ED is 10:1. This ratio drops only when physicians see and discharge patients.

The sooner patients are treated and discharged, the sooner the nursing ratio will drop to normal. Blocking patients in waiting rooms to protect an artificial 4:1 ratio inside harms patients, stops flow, and exacerbates overcrowding.

Stop Basing ED Care on In-patient Concepts

Emergency departments have to see everyone. When new sick patients arrive, they need to be seen right away. Because EDs can never say no to another sick patient, they operate on the assumption of *unlimited capacity*. However, many departments apply ideas from in-patient medicine to emergency care. We copy rigid concepts about rooms, stretchers, and individual providers and try to force them into a fluid service that must expand exponentially to see every unscheduled arrival. EDs cannot function with in-patient ideas; we need more elastic concepts. EDs need efficiency and resilience to meet patient needs.

Nursing Efficiency Challenges

Nursing efficiency raises a number of challenges. On the one hand, hospitals want to get maximum performance out of their biggest variable cost, nurses. On the other hand, nurses do not want to be taken advantage of; hence their powerful unions, which sniff around for signs of abuse and other illicit administrative acts.

As ED leaders, how can we align nurses' interests toward patient benefit and maximal efficiency in a salaried, heavily unionized environment?

It's not easy, but not impossible, because we can:

- Appeal to nurses' basic motivation for nursing – helping patients – and empower them to do so.
- Show how increased work now creates less panic later.
- Show that increased efficiency results in less work overall for the same number of patient visits.

Most nurses choose nursing because they want to help people. They enjoy patients and want to alleviate suffering. Nurse managers entered nursing for the same reasons. If managers show nurses that an ED process aligns with their fundamental motivation to care, most nurses will support it. Alignment empowers nurses. In fact, most nurses will work a bit harder and try new things if they can see that their efforts are directly benefiting patients.

But why would nurses support increased nursing efficiency? Efficiency does not seem to directly relate to patient outcomes or job satisfaction. It looks at clinical care at a meta level. It's complex. Change often requires teams to move toward a vision of care in which the details are not worked out. It requires a large amount of trust for nurses to follow, if they haven't been able to grasp all the details ahead of time.

Nurses need to see that getting patients in, seen, treated, and sent home quickly is directly tied to their best interests. Departments use patient volumes to determine nurse staffing. More nurses get hired when more patients attend an ED, regardless of how long patients spend in the department. It bears repeating that every hour a patient spends in the ED requires an hour of nursing care. If nurses can get patients home an hour sooner, they can save an hour of work for themselves. And patients want to be seen, treated, and sent home as quickly as possible. A win-win situation.

Create Resilience in Nursing

Teamwork and efficiency promise another major benefit for nurses. They create resilience. Working as fast as safely possible, and helping out colleagues whenever possible, frees up nurses' time to be ready for the next major medical disaster to arrive. Disasters require everyone to help out either directly or by covering their colleagues who get pulled in to helping with multiple traumas or a surge in volume somewhere else in the department. If nurses haven't built up resilience, haven't processed patients as quickly as possible, they return from helping with a trauma to critical tasks that have been left undone. Patients suffer, and nurses get dragged into the fallout. Teamwork means lending a hand; it means looking for opportunities to thin out the volumes in the ED.

Physicians require a similar approach; we'll return to them in step #5, on scheduling.

An Abundance Mentality vs. a Poverty Mentality

Leaders can ask staff, *How much more can you work? Do you work too much already?*

Emergencies demand *more*. Our EDs risk patients' health if they cannot respond to increased demand. Yet most departments run on a poverty mentality. They serve as many patients as possible doing as little as possible for each. Parsimony appears wise, even frugal, but it's backward and unsafe. A poverty mentality fosters a dysfunctional system with no resilience: nothing extra, no reserve for disaster, no teaching, no service excellence, no follow-up, only the bare minimum.

An abundance mentality, however, turns this situation on its head. Why not do as much as we can for every patient? Instead of sprinting through diagnosis and discharge, why not provide over-the-top care and service? Why not welcome patients back if they don't believe they can find great follow-up that works for *them*?

Abundance means treating all patients as if they were privileged. Privileged patients get all the extras without extending their stay.

Poverty delivers second-rate care and jeopardizes emergency services for the whole community. Abundance provides outstanding patient experience *and* builds resilience, the ability to flex and increase services on demand. Abundance is necessary to guarantee safe, quality care for the next wave of patients.

EDs back up everything else in the healthcare system – doctors' offices, out-patient clinics, imaging, and consultant services. *An abundance mentality guarantees that no matter what happens, patients will receive immediate, high-quality care.* EDs must create their own resilience with an abundance approach to service or risk their emergency preparedness for the whole community.

Make the Move to Unlimited Capacity

The 4 patients to 1 nurse rule on the other side of the triage dam artificially caps ED capacity inside. But if everyone providing care in and leading an ED were to accept that patient needs trump provider expectations and conventions, their ED would make a practical move toward *unlimited* capacity. Breaking the artificial and unsafe 4:1 rule means bringing patients inside so volume surges occur *inside* the department.

To handle surges of patients inside the department, teams must be flexible, think beyond rigid "assignments," help one another, and move resources seamlessly to the most impacted areas. Furthermore, surges are immediately visible to providers in care areas when patients are triaged *in* rather than *out*. Nurses and physicians work faster to maintain flow, calling for help as necessary.

While ratios sometimes rise above 4:1, often the reverse is true. There are only so many sick patients in one community, and nurses have found that an unlimited capacity approach actually decreases the total amount of nursing work. If enhanced flow carves two hours off the average length of a patient's stay, it carves hundreds of hours off patient care from the daily ED workload. Working hard during a surge decreases total work overall.

Nurse Concerns

A radical patient focus raises unique concerns for nurses. To get a first-hand nursing perspective for this section of this step, I interviewed nurse leaders at Southlake Regional Hospital and St. Joseph's Hospital. Some of these nurses worked as front-line staff in the *No More Lethal Waits* approach before working in management. A few of the leaders still work in these EDs, but most have been promoted or have retired. To avoid drawing attention to a particular nurse leader, the quotations stand without attribution. All quotations were only lightly edited. Most of the comments following the quotes are based on feedback from the nurses, too.

A Clear Goal: Put Patients' Interests First

"Departments need a really clear goal. Decisions need to be made with patient interests in mind, not nursing interests. Nurses are not the most important people in an emergency department, patients are."

There's a history of nurses being abused by administration, patients, physicians, and other providers. It's not surprising that nurses' feeling of *"You have no right to abuse us"* has been interpreted as *"We are more important than patients."* Leaders have to tread a delicate balance between making nurses feel valued and keeping patient interests front and centre.

"Many call it patient safety when they are just covering their own butt."

Always return to the question of whether patient interests are uppermost in nurses' minds. Are they just covering themselves or are they trying to do what's best for patients? When they complain and talk about *my licence* and *guidelines*, they are not focusing on patient interests. Do not back down.

What's Best for Triage vs. What's Best for Patients

One nurse educator said, *"Patients must be seen in 15 minutes according to CTAS (Canadian Triage and Acuity Scale). Triage is extra. If triage uses up more than the 15 minutes it takes to get a patient in front of a physician, it needs to be shorter. Patients want to see a physician, get a diagnosis, and get a plan of care."*

Another nurse manager said, *"Nurse leadership needs to take the bull by the horns. It will be better for nurses to get patients out of the department more quickly, so much safer."*

"Nurses must stop thinking that triage is safer."

"Thinning down triage does not mean cutting nurses; nurses just get moved inside the department to provide care there."

Nurses need enough doctors to see patients. It's far worse for nurses to try to see patients when there aren't enough doctors to help out.

"Getting patients straight in to the department doesn't mean there's no triage." Patients still need vitals if necessary based on their presenting complaint and general appearance. *"Nurses get very nervous about vitals."*

A machine can do vitals very quickly. Needing vitals does not mean giving patients a full assessment. If patients get straight inside, they need to get a full nursing assessment in a timely way inside. Nurses worry about someone coming back at them if assessments aren't getting done in a timely fashion inside the department.

Dealing with Nurses' Rules-based Culture

One leader pointed out how these changes challenge nurse leadership thinking. *"RNs are rules-based individuals."* They live and breathe policy and procedures. *"They aren't encouraged to be creative,"* she said. Getting used to the challenge to break the rules took six months at least.

Another nurse said, *"We don't allow RNs to get out, attend conferences, or explore professional leadership development."*

And this needs to change. *"They don't get exposed to new ideas. Not enough exposure to ideas. The whole world is looking at innovative ways to improve flow. Front-line RNs are siloed from the changes; they're unaware of what's going on in society. There are huge changes in other provinces and in remote areas, too."*

RNs find it hard to shift their thinking to *"doing what's right for the patient"* and doing it *"in the moment of."*

Ratios vs. Flexibility

"Nurse-to-patient ratios protect work speed. RNs resist floating around." For example, as a nurse leader put it, *"one nurse might have two empty beds on an assignment (out of four). Why can't she leave her partner with six patients for a short time, so she can go help out with a surge in another area? Doesn't happen."*

There is resistance *"to being flexible in the moment of need."* With respect to ratios, nurses want to know there are contingency plans if work gets too heavy. These include letting ratios expand for a while, or having a system of floating RNs to help, or a team leader who will come to help.

If nurses really push back on ratios, said one nurse, *"leadership should ask what the ratios are on the wards."* They should also ask, *"What's not going to happen with your patients if you go and help see other patients for a while?"*

"It requires servant leadership: I'll get you what you need to get your job done." Whether it's equipment or more staff, **"leadership needs to be seen as serving the nurses to help them perform to their best."**

Performance Management

"Slow nurses should be paired up with the go-getters." The efficient nurse can *"push the slow nurse along."* Nurses who do not pull their share of the load *"need to be asked to help out."* If they refuse, the nurse manager, or team leader, needs to be informed immediately, and to act on it.

Be certain to get clerical work done by someone other than nursing. *"Nurses sometimes like doing clerical work because it's easier than caring for patients."* Flow clerks can process admissions.

New Grads Need Time

New nursing graduates have much less diversity in their training. *"They require a full year of orientation to the ED."* They go through stringent training, but the training programs all have different philosophies of care: team based, primary independent nursing based, research focused, patient focused.

"Leadership doesn't know what they are getting."

Training used to be hospital based and RNs would leave training with ample experience across a wide exposure in the hospital. BScN trainees have little ability to flex in their thinking about ED process. *"RNs used to earn their merit based on their years of experience and hands-on exposure. Now, they come in without experience and only a BScN."*

Keep an Eye on the Data

Use department statistics to support the new process. It will show that RN hours can decrease when patients are processed more quickly. If the ED is understaffed, *"you must watch carefully that patients stay safe. Often leadership gets pulled to pay attention to other things."*

"Sometimes striking a separate staff committee designed only to keep an eye on the ED stats and performance will go far to increase staff confidence in management."

Leadership should keep the team looking at the value stream and asking whether long waits are right.

Primary Care vs. Team Nursing

"Primary nursing provides the safest care for the sickest patients." Ongoing assessment and care turns out better for patients. In

an ambulatory care setting, primary care nursing is less important, and teamwork supports patient flow.

"Nurses hated team nursing (officially)." They feel it isn't patient centred, that communication and documentation suffered, that reassessments were spotty and there was often no baseline assessment. They resisted any flexibility from their primary nursing style.

However, *"they now report 'we're all working together' whenever leadership checks on them."* So, *"they like to have it both ways depending on the patients."* For many aspects of care, *"they like to share work, but on their own terms."*

Steal Good Ideas

Leadership believes that *"the Studer approach, AIDET, 30/60/90 day interviews (what's great, what's good elsewhere) all help."* They *"steal as many good ideas as possible."*

"Discharge excellence is heavily promoted, as is patient feedback." Staff should know that patient concerns are encouraged and followed up on. Staff should be mandated to respond to patient concerns.

Partner with Unions

"Unions should not be given so much power." Work to partner with them, demonstrate you are doing the right things, and they will usually be very reasonable. *"Reassure them; keep them on the same page; guarantee the department is never unsafe."* Demonstrate contingency plans for workload; convince them.

Unionists *"want to prove they are needed and often work at being adversarial."*

A nurse in a hospital with an extremely strong nursing union said, *"In the old days, nurses would start and not even know who the union was or what it was concerned with. Today, the union rep meets with nurses on the first day of their orientation for a private interview."*

Most hospitals have union reps working clinically 75% of the time. *"At [one hospital], they've allowed the union reps to work on union issues full time."*

Get to the Physician Initial Assessment Faster

"Time to physician initial assessment helps nurses. It's the safest possible approach for patients, and nurses." Plus, the sooner patients get to see physicians, the sooner they go home.

"Complaints about PIA being only for physicians just deflects the discussion from the real issue: nurses have to work harder with short PIAs." Address the issue directly and put pressure where you need it.

Hire Well

Be very selective about nurse hiring. *"It takes years to build a team of nurses who really care about patients."*

Leadership needs to tell new hires to be prepared for *"high volumes, fast pace, high acuity, and multi-tasking, much more than they would with other EDs of similar volume."*

Overall, *"new RNs are very complimentary of the way patients flow through the department. They agree it's much better than the 10-hour waits seen in the past and that are common in other places."*

"They hate *how hard it was to get where we are now, but they agree with the results."*

They still complain about confidentiality and infection control, but appreciate the shorter waits.

Key Challenges for Nurses

- Break times need to be flexible, if patient needs come first.
- Having to help slower nurses.
- Nursing tasks get interpreted as demeaning to nursing autonomy and professionalism.

- Unlimited MDs can be called in for surges, but no RNs are on-call. Ideally, RNs should be available to call in, too.
- Chaos comes inside.
- This approach undermines the triage role. Loss of influence and control.
- Sacred cows: change undermines them…triage, RN-to-patient ratios, ED culture, the way it always was.
- Change management. People think they want it but wind up worked up over the way things used to be.
- Silo culture. There are limits to what can be fixed; nursing approaches on other floors cannot be overcome.

STEP# 4

Use Chairs and Exam Tables, Not Stretchers

L EADERS cannot ask staff to bring all patients inside the ED while continuing to use rigid, defined rooms or locations for each patient. At Southlake Regional (and the same was true for Dr. Duic when at St. Joseph's), we had to develop areas that (theoretically) could hold an unlimited number of patients in exactly the same way we used to expect waiting rooms to hold an unlimited number of patients. Now, only the sickest patients would own a care space. Stable patients waited for their tests, and had their treatments, sitting on chairs.

In other words, if your department brings all patients straight in, and only the very sickest get defined care areas, you need the right kind of furniture. Use the wrong furniture, and flow stops. You can determine which furniture to use for whom by the following rule: Keep vertical patients vertical, and moving. Any patient able to sit in a chair in the waiting room must never be made to lie on a stretcher. Traditional EDs break this rule all the time. They make patients wait for hours on hard chairs in crowded, chaotic waiting rooms until a comfy stretcher becomes available in a private room inside.

Break the Obsession with Stretchers

We had to break nurses' and physicians' obsession with stretchers at our hospitals.

Racing a patient through the emergency department on a stretcher makes for exciting TV. But for most EDs, stretchers are the enemy, because they clog patient flow. Most patients walk in to the emerg and walk home – less than 15% get admitted in Canada. There's no need to put patients on a stretcher unless absolutely necessary.

In a traditional ED, patients can wait for hours until they win the lottery, have their name called, and move out of the waiting room on their own stretcher. They get wheeled here and there on their stretcher, examined on it, and treated on it.

Doctors and nurses like stretchers. It is easier to find and examine patients who are on stretchers. Patients can be tucked in safe and sound, in the privacy and comfort of their own stretcher. Stretchers define capacity and give a clear sense of limits.

Stretcher locations are numbered and finite, no more than four stretchers to one nurse. When we run out of stretchers, we can close the door. No stretcher, no treatment.

For all these reasons, stretchers harm flow and delay life-saving treatment. They manifest the rigidity that prevents us from adapting to patient need. Stretchers facilitate inflexible nursing ratios, bed-blocking by admitted patients, and long patient waits.

Develop an Obsession with Tables

Patients without threat to life or limb, and who can sit, should proceed directly from triage to chairs inside. From there, they can be taken to exam rooms with examining tables. Sensitive discussions, and any care that requires privacy, happen in private exam rooms.

Patients must never stay in an exam room unless a clinician

is present. After patients are examined, they should be moved to chairs for IV treatment, or to wait for imaging and test results. Unlike the standard model, where patients stay in the same spot for examination and treatment, flow improves when patients get examined in one place, on an exam table, and have everything else done a few steps away as they wait on chairs. Spots to examine patients are a precious resource.

Exam tables differ from stretchers in several critical ways.

1 Exam tables have no wheels; thus, patients must walk to x-ray, or get taken in a wheelchair, which leaves the exam table free for other patients. EDs lose a care space when a patient gets pushed to x-ray on a stretcher.

2 Exam tables have paper, not sheets: physicians can quickly change the paper instead of waiting for housekeeping to change the sheets.

3 Tables are uncomfortable, so patients don't want to stay on them.

4 Tables have no sides, so providers cannot safely leave patients on them.

5 In-patient services cannot board patients on exam tables.

6 Stretchers are full in modern EDs, whereas tables are available for helping the next patient.

Patients sit for hours in most waiting rooms with serious or potentially life-threatening conditions. It is much safer to get them in and examine them on an exam table inside the ED, even if it means they have to sit on chairs during investigation and treatment.

Certainly, critically ill or incapacitated patients need stretchers for the duration of their ED visit. But for most patients, if they can walk, they can sit. And if they can sit, they do not need a stretcher.

Stretchers cause dysfunctional behaviour by:

1 Attracting admitted patients and boarding them for days.

2 Acting like real estate for ED patients; providers assign one "lot" to each patient.

3 Making patients immobile, even if they walked in to the ED.

4 Allowing providers to "tuck patients in," rails up, safe and sound.

Exam tables increase flow because they:

1 Remove a spot for admitted patients; exam tables are like operating room tables; OR tables are for surgery, not admission.

2 Provide a shared resource for all, not an assignment for one.

3 Get patients to move.

4 Keep providers moving with patients; exam tables are unsafe without a provider present, so patients spend minutes on an exam table instead of hours on a stretcher.

Dozens of patients cycle on and off one exam table, whereas one stretcher serves only a few patients per day. If the average patient spends six hours in the ED, each stretcher can serve, at most, up to four patients per day and usually much fewer.

As leaders, replace as many stretchers as possible with exam tables, if you haven't done so already. If exam tables are found only in the minor treatment area, you do not have nearly enough.

Like any change to historic processes, providers realize how attached they are to stretchers when leaders start asking them to use exam tables instead. But without building EDs twice the size, doctors and nurses cannot continue insisting that all patients, except the lowest-acuity ones, are to be seen on stretchers.

Staff support exam tables once they see how much they

improve flow. It is the best way to get patients seen and treated promptly in today's overcrowded EDs.

Stretchers ruin patient flow. They float around in a reservoir and promote dysfunctional behaviours. Get rid of stretchers wherever you can.

Change the Internal Furniture: ED Attitudes

EDs cannot function with the wrong furniture. But they also cannot function if teams have the wrong internal furniture – that is, the wrong attitudes. Here are a few things our team had to wrestle with to improve service and flow.

Get It Done Now

Process change requires supportive, engaged teams with great attitudes. Staff members set up patient expectations right at the front door. Without the right attitude, ED teams will never have a great department that consistently delivers outstanding service and high-quality outcomes. You might achieve great outcomes much of the time, but when it really matters, when you are stretched beyond coping, you won't live up to patient expectations.

More than anything else, emergency care providers must have a "get it done" attitude. It must start at the front door of the ED and infuse the whole department. *Get it done now.* Doctors and nurses should never have the luxury of waiting for scheduling or availability. Get it done now; get it done as quickly as possible. Emergency staff must get it done.

This feature makes emergency care stand out from all other parts of the hospital and separates emergency department care from other wards. It draws criticism and ire from others, but it's crucial for quality. Get it done now is about time, because time is a critical resource in the ED. Benefits include:

1 *A better quality-time relationship.* As discussed in step #1, timely service underlies quality service for much of ED care.

EDs must be structured and managed so every patient can be seen within a few minutes if necessary.

2   *Greater capacity.* As discussed in step #2, getting something done now frees up capacity for the next disaster coming through the door. EDs never have the luxury of relying on a scheduled break. They get to take breaks when all the work is done. Leaving a few tasks undone while providers get coffee or take a bathroom break could mean (a) the tasks never get done or (b) something terrible comes through the door and puts the whole department at risk.

3   *Better service to patients.* No one wants to spend extra time in a noisy, bright, commotion-filled ED. When at their lowest, sick patients want to get admitted to a ward or sent home. Delaying tests or treatment for *any* reason is not patient centred.

4   *Better fit with ED workers' skill set.* Getting things done now fits the way emergency providers are wired. "Make hay when the sun shines" defines how emergency staff view the world.

In many ways, in-patient medicine takes the opposite approach. Providers in this area have realized, after years of watching people's progress, that delay can be a good thing. They have seen that:

- Delay gives time for patients to get better.
- Time is what patients want when they're sick.
- Time shows compassion and politeness; rushing is rude.
- Most things can wait; why do today what can be put off until tomorrow?
- Sending patients home just means more work caring for the new patients waiting in line for the bed.
- Decisions made in haste are often wrong.
- Delay rarely kills anyone after a general diagnosis has been made.

Most staff in every other ward in the hospital will not fully understand or embrace a "get it done now" attitude. If EDs pretend to think like the medicine wards, ED patients will suffer.

Be Relentlessly Devoted to Serving Patients

Emergency staff get it done with a smile. Unlike in the operating room, where you can let your smile fade for a few hours behind your mask, or the radiology suite, where you can find a moment to turn off your public, customer-service attitude, in the ED there is *never* a time when you can turn off. Staff must commit to a relentless devotion to an attitude of customer service. Emergency providers should be the ones teaching other service industries how to provide outstanding customer service, not the other way around. Patients come to us at their moment of greatest need and usually when they are stressed and behaving poorly. We need to be there for them with the best care possible, but also with an approach that makes them believe their situation is the most important in the world at that moment.

Some nurses and doctors hate hearing this. Some also hate hearing that the customer is right, or that we should treat each patient in the ED as the most important. They say, *"How could this parent freaking out about a diaper rash be more important than the child who fell off a balcony?"*

No question: medically, socially, morally, in every way the second patient is more important than the first, except in the one way that matters most: the first patient believes they are the most important person in the ED at that time. Often patients with the most minor concerns have the highest levels of anxiety. We need to help them, too.

Who Decides the Validity of Patient Concerns?

Who determines whether patients' thoughts and beliefs are valid? This question strikes at the core of provider attitude. If a patient presents with what they believe to be a serious concern, should we treat it as such? If a patient thinks a broken finger-nail is the end of the world and we see things otherwise, do we have the right to treat them as though they have the seemingly insignificant concern that they report?

Who is right: we as providers, or our patients?

Until the whole ED team believes, truly believes, that patients' interpretations of their medical concerns are all that matters, we will never provide great service. As long as leaders support nurses and doctors who think it's okay to say things like, *"Come on! You'd think it was the end of the world! All they have is a broken toe!"* our departments will never provide great care.

By the time patients arrive for their visit, their expectations are running extremely high. For many, it may be the first time they have ever visited an emergency department. At that moment, they believe their concern is more important than anything else in the world. It is, for them, and they believe it should be for us. What could be more denigrating than to take their possibly once-in-a-lifetime event and tell them they shouldn't have even come to the ED?

Patients Are Always Right

At one time, *patients decided* whether their problem was worth a visit to the doctor. Patients were welcomed. Situations that turned out to be minor gave providers a chance to relax in an otherwise stressful day. But attitudes change. Nurses and doctors are taught that, instead of welcoming all patients and all complaints, they should judge whether patient complaints are deserving. With rampant specialization in medicine, prac-titioners are taught to refer to other specialists any patients with problems unsuited to their own highly specialized skills. Over time, providers develop strong opinions about who really needs their care.

ED workers have taken on the attitude that only the truly

sick patients "deserve" to be in the ED. Except for the critically ill, that is: ambulances should take those patients to regional centres. ED workers seem to want it both ways. They complain that patients with minor complaints should be treated in clinics, that critical patients should go directly to tertiary care, and that dying patients with advanced directives should never have been transported to the ED. It makes one wonder which patients, if any, would be sick enough, but not too sick, to meet ED physicians' and nurses' approval.

Here are some of the flags nurses and doctors use to identify undeserving patients. Undeserving patients:

1 Seek help for minor complaints that should have been handled at home.

2 Take poor care of themselves.

3 Attend the ED/clinic for their own convenience.

4 Demand repeat investigations.

5 Should be seen by their family doc, or public health nurse, or not at all.

Otherwise nice nurses and doctors adopt these attitudes. They reason that they're being a good steward of public funds and common sense. They confuse turning patients away with educating patients about options to access care. The words *"Let's face it: most patients don't need to be seen"* are all too often thought or said.

One thing is sure: "undeserving" patients don't get great care. *Ever.* We need a new attitude.

We need to always let patients define whether their concern is legitimate; to welcome all patients no matter how "minor" their complaint; to treat all patients as privileged, like family. Nothing less than new attitudes, ideals, and service standards – all based on a patient-centred philosophy – will do.

If we want to change the way patients access care, we need

to provide attractive options. We cannot provide a few, inconvenient options for access and then train providers to take a "send them away" attitude. This never promotes great service or care.

Changing minds will require changing incentives in our present system. We need redesign at the highest level. In the meantime, we need to change some common errors in how providers view patients.

Bucket Thinking Shames Patients

Nurses and doctors often think patients belong in buckets. Buckets of care: a primary care bucket, an emergency medicine bucket, an in-patient bucket...

It's clear that providers believe in a bucket concept of care when they:

1. Tell patients they're in the wrong bucket.
2. Tell patients to get out of the bucket.
3. Tell patients to go to a different bucket next time they need care.

Hotel management experts advise hotels to empower their staff to *handle any* issue that arises for guests during their stay.[33] Compare that with what often happens in healthcare:

- *"Sorry, ma'am, you'll have to go somewhere else for that."*
- *"Sorry, sir, I don't have time to discuss that with you. The ED isn't the place for that kind of problem."*
  - *Subtext: "And don't come back next time!"*

Funnel of Care

Patients should seek care where *they* choose to seek it. Increasingly, emergency departments act as access centres for medical care. Hours of debate could be saved by renaming North American EDs as Access and Emergency departments, or A&E. Private physician offices are unattractive for many patients, and no wonder: to go there for care they would have to fit acute concerns into rigid office hours, arrange for child-care, book time off work, and make multiple visits. EDs offer everything in one visit for most acute concerns, and even if things cannot be resolved in one ED visit, patients save time overall. Who can blame patients for attending?

Once patients present with a concern – no matter where they present – we should be prepared to help to whatever extent we can. Sending them away with a dismissive *"This isn't an emergency"* is unacceptable.

The funnel of care starts where patients choose to access care. It continues to more and more specialized care until patients get what they need.

With bucket-thinking, we expect patients to make their own clinical judgment. Then, we berate them for poor clinical judgment: *"Why didn't you go see the family-doc/walk-in-clinic/ anywhere-else?"*

Without clear, available access, patients are forced to attend the ED. EDs refer patients to their family docs for follow-up far more than family doctors refer patients to the ED, which is the opposite of what used to happen. Of course we *could* make the ED a referral-only facility like an ICU – no entry without a referral letter. Except that family docs and clinics would need advanced access, longer office hours, basic resuscitation equipment...

System issues force patients to seek care wherever they can get it. It's our job to help them when they get there, not send them away.

Lose the Arrogance

Many providers believe they are highly trained professionals who have earned respect. They demand high social standing and salaries to go along with it. They carve out expertise. They have skills. They stoop for no one.

Especially not patients.

Many patient concerns, by medical standards, are trivial. Especially in the ED, many concerns turn out to stem from anxiety or misinformation.

Changing thinking requires more than logic and argument. It demands courageous leadership. What happens when sports teams develop a bad attitude? How do teams recover when they're down?

- They can't call in new players.
- They can't increase the number of players on the field.
- They can't quit and go home.

How do they make the best of a losing situation?

When losers say, *"We'll never win!"* Leaders respond with, *"We can do this! We've beat this team before!"* When players drown out positive messages by screaming, "We'll lose!" that's when leaders speak up. They control the tone in the dressing room and on the field.

Striving for Excellence or Covering Our Butts?

While discussing overcrowding and "safe, quality care," a retired nurse manager said, *"It's all about doing what's best for the patients. People try to call it patient safety, but it's just covering your butt."* Motivations to help patients vs. protect ourselves start to compete when medicare runs short of money.

With enough resources, providers can protect themselves and focus on patient benefit. When resources dwindle, providers often have to choose between patient benefit and self-protection.

For example, (unfortunately) no one gets criticized for providing "really great care" inside an emergency department or on an in-patient ward. They claim they are patient-centred. But providers can spend as much time as they want with patients only if they make other patients wait for hours in the

ED waiting room or days admitted in ED hallways. Providers can champion ideal care settings – proper rooms, great infection control – only by forcing other patients to endure no bed, no quiet, and no infection control. This may be patient centred for some patients but certainly not for the waiting ones.

No one will fault a nurse or physician for working "really hard" and doing "a really good job" with patients – for being patient-centred by exploring psychosocial factors, attaining excellence in discharge processes, and educating patients.

As doctors and nurses, are we really working hard for patients or are we just covering our butts? Are we avoiding the risk of having to see a new patient in a less-than-ideal setting? Are we aiming for "faultless" care for our patient because we want what's best for patients or because we want what's best for us?

"But we're already at the 25th percentile for length of stay! What more can we do?" some may say. But even if your ED performs better than all the others, leaving patients to languish in hallways and waiting rooms goes against everything healthcare believes in. Emergency departments and in-patient services are guilty of the same thing: EDs leave patients in the waiting room; wards leave patients in the ED.

Our healthcare system does not have resources to allow providers to give a utopian vision of ideal care, all the time. Even if you don't have enough to give patients your best, you can still give them something; it's egregious to let them languish in the waiting room or ED.

Healthcare providers can describe their concerns in terms of quality, professionalism, or patient benefit without being patient-centred. When we make these comments in the face of unconscionable waits and suffering elsewhere – suffering that we could do something to alleviate – we are just covering our butts.

Scarce resources drive a wedge between providers, concerned about self-protection, and patients. With scarce resources, we protect ourselves at patients' expense. The system rewards this behaviour and creates an internal conflict between why we went into healthcare and keeping our jobs and livelihoods intact. With abundant resources, there's no conflict.

STEP# 5

Change Scheduling to Meet
Patient Needs More Efficiently

STREAMLINING the ED fails if patients are brought straight inside the ED and physicians don't see them rapidly for treatment. It does no good simply to move a crowd from one area to another. A crowd of patients waiting hours *inside* the ED to see a physician would create chaos; the security office would have to move inside the department from its usual home next to the waiting room.

As EDs change triage paradigms and nursing ratio expectations, they will also need to overhaul physician schedules, making them more responsive to patient needs than to arbitrary shift times.

Expect resistance. Like other shift workers, emergency physicians want predictability; they want defined hours on defined days. They like LEGO block schedules; they like to see schedules on grids, with little boxes in rows and columns. They like clearly defined start and stop times, so they know when they're working and when they're off.

But rigid shifts are provider centred, not patient centred. Rigid shifts work in industries where demand is scheduled and predictable. They fail in the ED, where the workload is unscheduled and variable. EDs will always struggle to meet patient needs if they do not adopt flexible scheduling with robust on-call systems.

The Problem with LEGO Block Schedules

Like most other sacred cows in medicine, scheduling operates primarily to meet provider needs. Doctors and nurses need a certain number of shifts to earn a desired income. They want shifts scheduled around the body's circadian rhythms and their social needs. Schedulers make a nod to patient flow by looking at historic patient volumes but not very often and not with much passion.

EDs need to build schedules around patient needs, first. Ideal physician (and nurse) schedules are ones that deliver the shortest possible patient waits and make the most efficient use of providers' time, preventing idleness. Of course, providers have needs, too, and these can be met with the approach described here.

Since most of the scheduling innovations at Southlake Regional and St. Joseph's have been done with physician schedules, this step focuses on physicians. However, the ideas you will find here can be used to redesign any staff schedule.

Typically, most schedulers, using a LEGO block approach to scheduling, guess how much work an average staff member can do, then schedule enough staff to meet the average amount of work each day. Schedulers see everyone as a block of identical size such that all blocks stack to create a wall that covers every hour of operation.

Individual productivity gets no consideration aside from casual attempts to stagger "fast docs" with "slow docs" on any given day. To build a schedule, schedulers plug staff in to a grid to meet the demands of an average day.

There are four problems with LEGO block scheduling:

- Nobody is average.
- No day is average.
- Understaffing makes patients wait.
- Overstaffing makes costs go up.

Average does not exist in clinical medicine. Treatment protocols can be standardized, but the core of clinical medicine – history-taking and physical examination – remains messy, relational, and often intuitive. Ask any emergency nurse: every doctor works at a different speed.

LEGO block scheduling guarantees long waits or over-staffing. Nurses know immediately whether a day will go well or poorly based on the doctor line-up for that day. Not because some doctors are poor clinicians, but because the overall grouping of physicians on any day determines productivity. A line-up of the nicest physicians, if they aren't accurately matched to the anticipated patient volumes for that day, creates chaos. Patients and staff suffer for it.

Discussing speed is controversial in EDs. Slow providers say fast ones are slipshod and careless. Fast providers say slow ones are lazy or talk too much. Schedulers try to avoid this minefield. It's safer to assume average work speed, and hope patients won't wait and costs won't soar.

But patients wait...and costs soar.

The Problem with Adding More Shifts

What is the standard administrative response to long waits to see a physician? Most leaders watch until average patient wait times climb unacceptably high and then add more physician shifts. Some get sophisticated enough to add extra shifts only on days that historically have higher volumes, for example, Mondays.

Adding extra shifts helps, but it is a clumsy approach. Administrators must keep close watch on the balance between patient wait times and physician idleness. Long patient waits make patients and nurses angry and stressed. Too much idleness wastes money in a salaried setting, or drives down physician remuneration in fee-for-service settings.

At this point, many attack fee-for-service. *"It's just physician greed. There'd be no waits if physicians weren't so concerned about their billings."* This is true of all workers.

No patients would wait if every able-bodied ED nurse, technician, and support staff came to work caring nothing about pay, willing to work for free. Nursing shortages would disappear if nurses stayed late and worked a few extra hours or skipped their breaks or came in on their day off without pay. Think how wonderful it would be for patients to have an unlimited supply of altruistic MDs and nurses.

But of course nurses, techs, clerks, and physicians all work for an income. Physicians do not want to work for free any more than unionized, salaried workers do. However, adding more shifts to solve wait times requires an enormous number of nurses and physicians and increased funds to pay them. If cost was no concern, each day could be staffed based on the highest-anticipated volumes, not the average. Even then, an ED could be overwhelmed, but much less often.

Is there a way to maximize efficiency with physician scheduling while creating the shortest possible patient waits?

There is. The solution lies in matching MD productivity with historic patient volumes and patient waits in real time. This requires measuring or having a sense of three things: physician productivity, daily patient volumes, and in-the-moment patient wait-time data. The first two of these are discussed in what follows; the third is the main subject of step #7.

Issues with Physician Productivity

We need to reframe provider "speed." Dr. Marko Duic's view is that every physician has a number of patients he can safely see per hour. "Ask any nurse how many patients a physician sees in an hour," he says, "and they will tell you as accurately as reading a number off the doctor's forehead." Everyone can see the physicians' number, but the physicians cannot see their own number.

We cannot change the speed people work. Ideally, all workers should be welcomed onto the schedule, regardless of how fast or slowly they work. Schedulers rely on an intuitive sense of clinician speed to create a schedule that minimizes patient waits without wasting physician time.

But what if some providers do not want to work at their maximum speed? What if they want to work at a more leisurely pace, if they had the choice?

Also, some patients require far more time than others. Mayer and Jensen suggest that we "do fast things fast, and slow things slow."[34] What if a number of slow patients cluster on a particular day?

How can we build a schedule that minimizes patient waits *and* maximizes staff efficiency? And how can we get staff to want such a schedule?

American hospitals understand and value MD efficiency. Canadian hospitals? Not so much. Canadian physicians are not paid out of the hospital budget, so hospitals worry about physician efficiency only if it impacts hospital budgets or performance.

Physician time is the most valuable resource in your department. It costs the most, requires the most training, and should be the rate-limiting step on every process. Privately run hospitals are so obsessed with physician efficiency that they track every footstep and pause using computerized real-time locating services (RTLS, aka Radio Frequency Identification, RFID). An efficient ED keeps physicians busy doing things that only physicians can do, all the time.

This goes against everything written in the hidden curriculum for hospital administrators in Canadian medicare.

Hospitals know their bottom line improves by transferring as many duties as possible to physicians. If hospitals can save money by getting a physician to perform work that otherwise would require the hospital to hire staff to perform, administrators support it. Unless the idea promises to cause war with the unions, administrators will always strive to give physicians as much unpaid work as possible.

Resist this.

Even if you are reading this as a hospital administrator, you will lose, in the end, by continually pushing work off hospital budgets and on to physicians. Doctors will be more devoted, more enthusiastic, and more likely to recruit their best colleagues if word gets out that a particular hospital values physician efficiency.

Just as physicians should only do medical work, physicians must never be idle. They should always be adding value for patients and the department. Idleness may even be worse than performing tasks better done by non-physicians, except for the fact that some physicians like to be idle now and then. Idleness by choice can be supported, just don't reward it. Many departments remunerate idle physicians at the same rate as productive physicians.

Don't do it.

Rewarding idleness eats away at the fabric of a team. No doubt, when a group bills against a pooled fund, there's a balance between rewarding physicians who scramble to see patients and physicians who scramble for coffee breaks. Groups need to work this out on their own. However, idleness, per se, must always be seen as wasteful. Resting, reviewing labs, teaching residents, or any other necessary function do not count as idleness. Be alert to physician idleness wherever it shows up, and be relentless in stamping it out.

Daily Patient Volumes

Other businesses figured this out ages ago. Many industries provide great service even though they have no guarantee how much service will be required that day.

Take restaurants, for example. The good ones adjust their wait staff to meet unscheduled, fluctuating demand. If more diners arrive than usual, these restaurants call in more waiters. On slow days, waiters leave early. On days when the most efficient waiters are working, fewer get scheduled. More staff work on days scheduled with slow waiters. Schedules benefit customers, not wait staff, and deliver the highest-possible efficiency.

Like waiters, physicians work at different speeds vis-à-vis patient volumes. Unlike waiters, they don't always know when they need to speed up: when EDs hide patients in waiting rooms, physicians have little sense of patients' rate of arrival.

With clock-based shifts, physician capacity cannot adapt to changes in patient volume and acuity. As with restaurants, great service demands flexible start and stop times.

But how do you balance the three equally important, competing goals of shorter patient waits, predictable shifts, and greater physician productivity? These goals create a trilemma. A trilemma exists when only two out of three things can be true at the same time.

The classic trilemma joke from the Soviet era goes like this: "God comes to the Soviet people and says: 'I will give each of you a choice of three blessings in life, but you can only have two out of the three. You can be an honest person, you can be a smart person, or you can be a member of the Communist Party. If you are smart and honest, then you cannot be a Communist. If you are a smart Communist, then you cannot be honest. And if you are an honest Communist, then obviously, you must not be very smart.'"[35]

The scheduling trilemma looks like the following, in which you are to choose two of three options.

1 Timely patient assessment.

2 Clock-based start and stop times.

3 Efficient utilization of physician time.

You cannot have all three when workload is highly variable. One of these goals must be partially sacrificed to achieve the others. Patient-focused care demands timely assessment. Timely assessment using rigid, clock-based scheduling requires overstaffing. Overstaffing wastes EP time during slow periods. If timely assessment is essential and efficient use of physician time is a priority, then EP schedules must be demand-based and flexible rather than clock-based and rigid.

The only way to minimize patient waits and maximize physician efficiency is to use flexible shift times based on immediate patient demands.

Scheduling Nirvana

Imagine a schedule where you could work any day you wanted, see as many (or as few) patients as you wanted, and take as many holidays as you wanted.

Sound unbelievable?

Dr. Marko Duic has honed a physician-scheduling system that delivers MD choice, MD control, and a perfect fit between physician speed and patient volumes. He shares how he does it in the following interview.

Is it true that you've figured out a way to give physicians choice, control, and as many holidays as they want?

For individual physicians, it's true. The only restriction is that a few physicians need to stick around to keep the emerg going – so not everyone can take off at the same time. This might be an issue if everyone in the department wants to go to the same conference. But if an individual physician wants to go off for three to six months, say, to cycle from Cairo to Cape Town, it's not a problem.

How long have you been doing this?

Since 2001.

How do the physicians like it?

They state that it's a major reason why they'd never go to another ED to work.

How do patients like it – what results have you achieved?

The most important patient satisfaction correlate is their time to see the doctor [Physician Initial Assessment time]. Well, the two hospitals [St. Joseph's and Southlake] in Ontario that use this system are often number 1 and number 2 in PIA times, and one of them is definitely a leader in satisfaction among peers.

What do the nurses think of this system?

At first they weren't that pleased that we could muster *up any* number of *physicians any* time, and they would get stuck with a pile of orders. They had to see that a pile of orders is better than a pile of unseen patients. At least with the patients having been seen by MDs, nurses could be asked to do the most urgent orders first. What the nurses like about this system is that there are always enough doctors to see the patients, so they never have to get abused by impatient patients. There's never a day when three slow physicians work back to back and the place explodes.

Could this system work anywhere? Do you think you could teach others to do it?

Of course it could work anywhere. It's how patients would schedule doctors, if patients were allowed to schedule us.

Most emergency departments schedule a fixed number of shifts every single day, but you don't. Why?

Each physician has a number of patients per shift that he's most comfortable seeing. It could be 15, could be 30, could be 45, could be 60. And each emergency department has a number of patients that they see any given day. So, for example, in one of our departments, we see 300 on Sundays and Mondays and 270 the other five days. So I have to schedule enough physicians that their combined capacity to see patients adds up to the number of patients I'm expecting. So if all the fast guys go on a conference together, the slow remaining guys have to be scheduled in larger numbers – maybe 9 or 10 of them in a given day – to see that many patients. If the slow guys go on a conference, I might only need five or six of the remaining fast guys to see the patients. If everyone's in town, and I alternate fast and slow guys, I might need seven or eight physicians. If the physicians work at different speeds, how can you expect to have the same number of them per day?

How do you determine exactly how fast each MD works?

I have stats, but they don't really work that well. So I do it by trial and error, repetition, and intuition.

But what if more patients arrive on a particular day?

Shifts start when patient waits get up to a certain level. Physicians call each other to figure out when the next one needs to show up. If the day's busier, it becomes evident in the conversations. Physicians come in early, and stay late, and if needed, call in an extra physician.

And what if you need another physician to help?

We use our on-call funds to pay one of them to show up. We call in turn, alphabetically, and change the order by one physician each time, so everyone gets a chance.

Who decides if more MDs are needed on any given day?

The physicians who are working in the department at the time. If they risk running over the target patient waiting time, they call extra help in.

What if the physicians working that day do not call for extra help?

Then the times go over, this is a disaster, and they need to explain why they didn't.

What are your thoughts on the provincial Hospital On-Call funding system?

It's good to have money to pay physicians to come in to serve patients, especially in the ED, where volumes and acuities are unpredictable, and where timely access to care is what's held out to the public in the name that's posted on the door: Emergency Department.

Are there times when you have scheduled too many MDs on one day? What happens then?

They either shorten all the shifts, or cancel one of them, or both. They come to an agreement that suits them all.

Okay, let's focus on the mechanics of schedule creation. How do physicians pick their shifts?

They submit a selection form that shows me when they want to work, when they can work, when they would prefer not to work, and when they cannot work. I use all the physicians' forms to give everyone a schedule that's almost entirely made up of shifts they want or can do.

Is it completely different every month?

Basically, yes. Some patterns repeat – some like nights; others like Wednesday mornings; some people can never work Friday evenings. But overall, it's different every month.

What happens if there are too many shifts requested by the group?

Everyone gets a bit less than they asked for.

What happens if you cannot provide enough coverage to meet the expected volumes on a day?

Short-term, everyone works a bit more than they would like. Long-term, hire more people. But if it's one day, and no one wants to work then, then there's a lottery.

Can MDs take holidays?

Yes, any time, for any length of time. We've had people take full-year sabbaticals or four-to-six-month LOAs and come back to a full shift roster. This system is totally flexible. Twenty doctors can cover the absence of one or two for a long time with minimal disruption.

What if everyone wants to take holidays at the same time?

Then we close the department. No, seriously, there's a

max of about one-third of the department who can be on holidays for a longer period, or half of the department for a few days, or two-thirds for a day or two, and it can still have full staffing.

What about Christmas, New Year's, and summer vacation – how do you handle those holiday requests?

In whatever way the physicians want, but, overall, some people always want to work them, and if there aren't enough, then there's always the record of who did it last year and the year before – those people get first dibs on taking them off this year.

Physician Efficiency

To achieve maximum physician efficiency, leaders need a great schedule *and* flexibility. You need to match demand with productivity and create hour-to-hour flexibility.

Regarding the former, determine how many patients attend your ED per hour. You know how fast your docs work. Schedule enough MDs, based on their individual work speeds, to meet the average patient volumes by hour. Some days may require twice as many doctors, if all the MDs happen to be slower that day. Practically, you create the schedule following these steps:

1 Determine the average rate and volume of patients seen by each physician.

2 Estimate how many patients the department sees per day.

3 Let physicians chose whatever shifts they want and collect their shift preferences. (Choice makes doctors happy.)

4 Have physicians indicate 50% more desirable shifts than the total they want for whatever time frame you are scheduling (e.g., one month).

5 Use 1–3 above to create a schedule that matches demand with productivity.

6 Provide *approximate* shift start times.

Even the best schedule will never compete with all the changes in unscheduled patient visits.

As for creating hour-to-hour flexibility, physicians must stay late, arrive early, go home early, or call in more MDs for help when patient volumes warrant. Let the physicians on duty control these decisions, and keep them accountable for the outcomes.

Hour-to-hour flexibility should largely be the responsibility of doctors, as described in detail in the next step.

STEP# 6

Give MDs Responsibility for Flow and Hire Patient Navigators

Give MDs Responsibility for Flow

Patient arrivals will ruin the best scheduler's attempts to have enough physicians working without wasting their time with idleness. Every day, at some point during the day, patient volumes will decrease such that there are too many doctors working in the ED. At other times – more common than slow times in most departments – patient volumes will overwhelm physicians, and wait times will climb.

Leaders can build hour-to-hour flexibility by developing flexible start and stop times for shifts, and by creating a robust on-call system.

Build and Operationalize the Schedule

Flexible shift times link directly with the scheduling approach described in the previous step, "Change Scheduling to Meet Patient Needs More Efficiently." With a great schedule in hand, physicians responsible for patient flow will always outperform approaches that make flow the concern of someone other than the physicians working on shift that day.

Physicians need to monitor and be empowered to change staffing levels within minutes of changes in patient volumes and acuity. It should be a normal part of everyday work in EDs.

At Southlake Regional and St. Joseph's, we use the following approach to build physician-staffing flexibility into every day, just like restaurants have been doing for years:

1 Physicians are given *approximate* shift start times.

2 The most recently arrived physician functions as charge physician, monitoring patient wait times.

3 A few hours before each shift, the next physician due to arrive calls and speaks to the most recently arrived (charge) physician to negotiate an *actual* start time based on patient waits.

4 If wait times threaten to exceed the target, the charge physician calls the next incoming physician in early, asks the outgoing physician to leave later, or activates the on-call physician.

5 On slow days, the charge physician tells the incoming physician to start later and the outgoing physicians to leave earlier, and considers cancelling part or all of a shift (the last option tends to pertain later in the day).

Leaders need real-time data and close feedback to help physicians learn this new process. We discuss data more in the next step, "Use Real-Time Data and Adopt a Full Capacity Protocol."

Naturally competitive physicians take to this flexible approach. They love being able to do something about patient flow instead of just moving from patient to patient while trying to ignore the chaos around them. They want to help. Give physicians responsibility and control over ED patient waiting and flow.

Eager to Be On-Call – Seriously?

Despite a scheduler's best efforts, patient volumes sometimes swamp the team working that day. Even after calling everyone in as early as possible, patients keep coming, and wait times lengthen. Most on-call programs work so poorly, they aren't even worth mentioning here.

How can you make on-call so attractive that physicians get into fights because they were not called in when they should have been?

If doctors find being at home more attractive than dropping what they are doing and rushing in to help see hordes of waiting patients, your call system will fail. Most approaches to on-call pay physicians a few hours' worth of income to be available and a small premium for the first few patients seen. Physicians weigh the costs and benefits and try very hard to stay home by being hard to reach and debating whether there's really a need for extra help.

Find the Tipping Point

Everyone has a price. At some point, everyone would find the benefits of coming in to help on a day off greater than staying at home.

Leaders need to find that point.

For most physicians, paying them double what they would otherwise make on a full shift will tip their attitudes. Physicians will fight to come in if they know that, just for showing up, no matter how long or short they stay, they will get at least as much as they would make on a whole shift. All of a sudden, they will answer their phones on the first or second ring, even at 0300. You will never be short of extra help.

But if getting called for being on-call is like winning the lottery, where do you get the lottery money?

Fundraising requires a set of skills all of its own. At worst, each member in your group can contribute to a pool to fund on-call. Better yet, try to get additional outside funds for your group from grants, educational stipends, drug studies, hosting conferences, recruitment funding, or government programs. Members appreciate any value you can add.

An on-call system must benefit patients or be scrapped. Expect to pay on-call physicians in the same way that hospitals pay double-time to staff in special circumstances or that hospitals pay nurses and operating room staff even if cases are cancelled.

Who Calls? How Do You Prevent Abuse of the System?

The charge physician, the one responsible for ED flow at the time of need, must activate the on-call. Fellow physicians in the department should take part in the discussion, and charge nurses and administrators may be involved, too.

When wait times or patient volumes balloon, the charge physician should discuss the situation with his colleagues in the department. Do they have enough manpower to meet patient demand? Have they extended physician shifts? Do they need to call another physician in to help?

Unbalanced incentives to call for help may create dozens of calls and bankrupt the on-call system in the first week. Incentives drive behaviour. Leaders need to balance the ease of calling for help with some incentive for physicians to work harder and stay late. For our groups, paying out unused funds from the on-call pool to the overnight shifts provided the right balance. Giving unused call money to those who worked overnights during the year (based on the number of shifts worked) achieves a number of things. It:

- Makes night shifts very attractive.
- Encourages physicians to work harder in the moment to maintain short wait times.
- Still provides a meaningful on-call support for patient flow.

Sometimes physicians refuse to activate the on-call system, knowing that the unused funds will come to them in the end anyway. Leaders need to maintain watch on the wait times every day. When waits go up, physicians working that day need to be asked what they did to fix the situation. Why did they fail to activate the on-call system? If a pattern of longer waits forms around particular physicians, more shifts need to be scheduled when they work. So, too, if on-call gets activated whenever they work.

Use Patient Navigators

Beyond process and patient flow, patient navigators (PNs) offer the next biggest improvement to efficiency. Working with physicians in a 1:1 ratio, they improve physician output by at least 20%, and, in a particularly inefficient ED, often much more. Physicians who choose to work with a PN hire and pay the PN. PNs function more like personal assistants than salaried hospital union members.

Emergency physicians spend more time looking for charts, finding lab reports, and checking if treatments are done than they do caring for patients. After continual interruptions from allied health providers, patients, and other physicians, doctors have little time left for patients.

PNs free physicians to provide what patients want most: time with their doctors. This improves quality by allowing MDs to focus on patients rather than on collecting patient histories and performing clinical examinations. Time spent by physicians doing anything other than helping patients is wasted time.

We tried scribes at Southlake and St. Joseph's but found our greatest need was not transcription but navigation. Patient navigators do two main things:

1 Direct physician–patient traffic.

2 Manage information.

They do not make clinical decisions, give clinical advice, or order clinical care. PNs improve:

1 Patient experience.

2 Physician efficiency.

3 Team communication, especially between nurses and physicians.

PNs perform non-medical tasks that MDs do when working without a PN. They do anything doctors do that does not require a medical degree. We use patient navigators to:

1 Keep the team informed of patients waiting in all areas of the department and find out which patients are waiting to be seen next.

2 Accept and photocopy patient handover lists from the physician handing over and make sure the patients on these lists are reviewed and looked after by the accepting physician.

3 Keep track of all the patients their doctor has seen and when patients are ready for reassessment.

4 Obtain the chart of the next patient for the next available MD to see.

5 Access electronic charts; print out reports.

6 Prepare charts for MD reassessment.

7 Get bloodwork, x-rays, etc. printed and ready to hand to patients at discharge.

8 Update MD data in the ED information system (tracking board).

9 Page and receive specialist phone calls.

10 Receive and manage other incoming calls and hold non-critical calls for their MD when their MD is with a patient.

11 Help RNs locate MDs for urgent needs.

12 Inform patients about wait times and reasons for them.

13 Direct patients in and out of examination stations.

14 Update RNs on their MD's work plans.

15 Receive RN requests for patient reassessment.

16 Work with the team (e.g., RNs and RTs) to gather equipment for procedures.

17 Follow the rules and regulations of the hospital.

18 Hand out patient information sheets and referral forms to patients when instructed by MDs.

19 Enter patient areas as appropriate to receive their MD's instructions or give phone to MD.

20 Hold non-critical calls for MDs.

21 Assist with paperwork to ensure proper completion.

22 Create handover list at the end of a shift.

Ideally, PNs are non-unionized contract workers who do all the non-medical tasks physicians are expected to perform.

Again, PNs increase MD efficiency by at least 20% and sometimes much more. They easily pay for themselves while adding priceless improvements to quality and physicians' work experience.

PN Pitfalls

Like all staff, navigators come with their own personalities, skills, and level of emotional intelligence. PNs rarely excel at everything. Here are some of the issues we've had to manage:

1 *The PN job description must be clear.* Clerical and nursing unions smell blood at any new provider in the department. They want to bring everyone under their set of rules for behaviour and (non)productivity. They will accuse PNs of taking their work even though the services PNs offer are not part of clerks' and nurses' job descriptions.

2 *Communication must be clear.* Nurses hate being told what to do, especially by navigators. They bristle when navigators relay any messages. It is best to have MDs speak directly to RNs, or write orders down. Delivering a handwritten order softens delivery and protects PNs from attack.

3 *Patient confidentiality must be stressed.* Coming in to a clinical environment highlights many of the behaviours providers take for granted having trained and worked with patients for years. PNs need reinforcement of basic things like: patient privacy, knocking before entering (better yet, to knock and ask, *"Are you covered?"*), and never looking at records of family or friends.

4 *Boundaries need to be set.* By nature PNs are eager to help, which can get them into trouble when physicians ask, in desperation, *"I need some Epi! Stat!"* and no one moves. Experienced PNs will know what's being asked for, where it is, and how to get it. They might place it on the table beside an RN who's ignoring the MD as she focuses on her charting, or they might offer it to the RN. Either way, they are taking a big risk.

Patient Navigator Job Description

Feel free to use the following job description in your own hospital's Rules and Regulations. This description puts the 22-item list from above into language found in hospital R&Rs, adding two at the end. The description is followed with a list of what PNs do and do not do and a summary of the purpose of PNs.

Patient navigators work with one doctor per shift. They assist the doctor by performing a variety of non-medical tasks that the doctor usually does while on shift. They do anything doctors do that does not require a medical degree. As such they:

1 Keep informed of patients waiting in all areas of the department and inform doctors which patients are waiting to be seen next.

2 At the beginning of a shift, accept and photocopy the handover list from the physician handing over; make sure all these patients are reviewed and looked after by the accepting physician.

3 Keep track of all the patients doctors have seen and when patients are ready for reassessment.

4 Obtain the chart of the next patient for the next available MD to see.

5 Access physician portal for MDs and print out necessary reports.

6 Attempt to obtain the necessary reports from physician portal for the MDs to refer to prior to seeing their next patient.

7 Prior to patient reassessments, print off blood-work and x-ray results and put them on the patient charts for the doctors to give to their patients.

8 Keep their doctor's tracking board on the departmental computer up to date.

9 Call locating to page specialists and receive calls from them.

10 Receive all incoming calls for their physician, passing on to the physician what they need to deal with at that time.

11 Help nurses find doctors to get approval for orders, EKGs, and so on.

12 Keep patients informed about wait times and reasons for wait times.

13 Direct patients to examination stations and direct them back to waiting areas after assessment.

14 Keep nurses informed about where their doctor is and is going next.

15 Receive reports from nurses about when patients require a reassessment.

16 Work with the team (e.g., RNs and RTs) to gather equipment required for procedures, including procedures requiring sedation.

17 Follow the rules and regulations of the hospital, e.g., code of conduct, rules of confidentiality.

18 Hand out patient information sheets and referral forms to patients when instructed by their MD.

19 Enter patient examination areas when appropriate to receive instructions from their MD or to give phone to the MD.

20 Hold non-critical calls for their MDs when MD is with patients.

21 Make sure doctor fills out paperwork properly for patient tests and assist with this.

22 Create a handover list at the end of a shift.

23 Will be respectful of all interprofessional members of the ED and expect to be treated in the same way.

24 Do all of it with good humour and positive attitude in a polite and semi-invisible way.

Patient Navigators do not:

1 Leave their physician during their shift without prior conversation. They always know where their physician is, and physicians always know where their patient navigator is. If PNs are capable of losing their physician, they are not paying sufficient attention most of the time.

2 Come late or leave early from a shift without prior conversation with and agreement from their physician. They stay until their physician's work is done.

3 Make personal phone calls, send texts and emails, or conduct other personal business unless their physician has cleared this and are fully engaged with patients during this time.

4   Sit while the physician they are with is standing – not out of respect but out of practicality. If the physician is writing at a bedside table in the hall, it's not efficient for the patient navigator to hand the physician information while sitting in the nursing station – particularly if the patient navigator is distracted by conversations with other clerks or by personal business on the computer or phone.

5   Give medical advice to patients.

6   Perform clinical assessments of patients.

Thus the overall purpose of the patient navigator position is:

1   To improve the quality of patient experience.

2   To improve the efficiency of the physician.

3   To improve communication between members of the healthcare team, especially nurses and physicians.

STEP# 7

Use Real-Time Data and Adopt a Full Capacity Protocol

Real-Time Data in Minutes, Not Averages in Hours

If ED teams want great performance, they need to know wait times reported in minutes. Average wait times will not work. Wait times reported at 10 a.m. and 2 p.m. will not work. Leaders need to know how their department functions every hour, down to the minute. Just as managers need an operations report and board members need a budget, so do ED leaders need wait times reports, in minutes, every hour.

Don't Rely on Average Wait Times

"Average" causes patient suffering. Touting averages in healthcare is like reporting the average number of parachutes required for passengers to jump from a plane.

Data drive healthcare management. Everyone has become an amateur quant (quantitative analyst). But we often use the wrong data. Leaders gush and fawn over data from the last quarter. We get excited about improvements, anything we can share with the board. But last quarter's data mean nothing for patients getting care today and providers who have to function with patients in front of them. Providers are not excited about data from last week, yesterday, or even from this morning. Providers need data that are relevant now.

Healthcare needs live data to be provided the way a thermometer provides data. Patients benefit when providers change their behaviour based on feedback received from data that inform them about the immediate circumstance. Yesterday's information helps – if clinicians can remember what they did yesterday. They will remember horrendous cases or surges in volume from yesterday. But they will never remember the thousands of banal decisions made that truly impacted performance. This information resides in the background of thinking, safe from examination.

Change happens when data become available in the moment. Hour-by-hour data can pinpoint who worked at a particular time and what care was given.

Real-time data allow leaders to query performance and address it immediately. At first, physicians and nurses do not enjoy being asked why things are slowing down, why waits are creeping up. But very quickly, they realize that leadership cares about performance and flow, and that they can often help improve flow in the moment instead of leaving it all up to providers.

Ask your data analytics support team to report waits every hour, in minutes. Hourly reporting supports, or corrects, hunches about when wait times lag. With the right data, you can start innovation. What gets measured, changes.

Leaders also need a daily performance report. Average wait times, average patient volumes, and average provider work speed mean nothing to a patient standing in line with tearing chest pain. Leaders should be upset when they hear averages reported, or at the very least, should ignore them. Average means nothing if it allows patients to die at the extremes. In a high-risk environment like the emergency department, we need information about the worst performance, when the system is overwhelmed.

Drive Change with Patient Satisfaction Data

Patient satisfaction data drive change. This information gives leaders the credibility they need to start and sustain new processes.

Immediate feedback on patient experience means more than last year's average. Smart providers look for feedback "in the moment of" by asking about service, and doing service recovery before patients leave. Some organizations call patients within 24 to 72 hours of their visit to ask about service.

However, most patient satisfaction reports come from large surveys collected using standardized questions that compare institutions. Despite their limitations, patient satisfaction data do provide energy to fuel change. Terrible results demand change; nurses and doctors cannot dismiss low patient satisfaction. They want to support change that improves patient satisfaction. (If they don't, maybe they need a performance meeting?)

What if your ED performance is above average? Even worse, what if you are the best performing hospital in the comparison, but you think you still need change?

Hospitals love to be the fastest turtle. This is why teams need to have their own definition of great patient care. They need to come up with their own understanding of what great patient satisfaction might look like beyond what standardized surveys indicate. At Southlake, we thought "treating patients like family" captured the essence of what we hoped to achieve for every patient. If we held ourselves to that standard, we could interpret patient satisfaction results in light of a larger vision, and use the same frame to direct improvements when scores were low.

Decrease Length of Stay

ED teams have only partial control over many things that impact patient length of stay. For instance, laboratory and diagnostic imaging turnaround, consultant response, and house cleaning have a huge impact on the efficiency of a department. But aside from gaining influence by building relationships with the people who provide these services, EDs have little control over their performance.

EDs have even less leverage with services outside the ED that impact length of stay. In a publicly funded system with powerful unions, simply assigning accountability by posting performance may be the best way to encourage change in the other services you depend on for flow, such as in-patient length of stay, hospital discharge times, and the time it takes to transfer a patient to ward by department

Of the myriad issues that increase patient length of stay, it would make sense for ED leaders to focus on what they *can* control: ED nurse and physician behaviour. For the most part, closing the waiting room and getting patients straight inside the department will immediately decrease length of stay. This move helps nurses and physicians to feel patient volumes directly and change work patterns to match them. Also, patient navigators can help doctors focus on prompt patient reassessment and increase efficiency overall.

Your strongest position, by far, comes from demonstrating a relentless commitment to doing everything in your power to improve patient experience in your own department without blaming your poor performance on everyone else. Which brings us to the importance of adopting a Full Capacity Protocol.

Adopt a Full Capacity Protocol

It's Hospitals That Make Patients Wait

Early in 2014 the *Globe and Mail* published the article "Canada's ERs Missing Mark on Waiting Times, New Statistics Reveal."[36]

The *Globe* got it wrong. Hospitals, *not* emergency departments, leave patients in overcrowded EDs for nearly 30 hours, before moving them to an in-patient bed. EDs do not make admitted patients spend too long in the ED. Hospitals use EDs as extra capacity to keep their in-patient areas calm and orderly.

Hospitals choose to leave extra patients admitted in the ED. They could spread patients out over all the in-patient wards. But very few hospitals enter the political battle of angering unions by placing extra patients in in-patient hallways, despite the nearly 400 published articles showing that mortality and morbidity increase for every hour admitted patients are warehoused in EDs.[37]

Full Capacity Protocols empty EDs,[38] have been used in Canada, and leave no excuse for exposing patients to the proven risks of long waits in the ED. Until government changes incentives so hospitals start saving lives by getting admitted patients out of EDs, we will not see an end to over crowded emergency departments.

Why Hospitals Overcrowd EDs

Please do not use what I'm saying as ammunition for complaining to your hospital administration. While emptying the ED of admitted patients has been done successfully all over North America, saving lives in the process, your senior team has competing needs to address. If they choose to decrease the useable size of your department by leaving it full of admitted patients, they probably have a good reason for doing so.

In fact, hospitals all too often choose to board patients in emergency departments, or, rather, they choose not to remove admitted patients from the ED. If senior administrators wanted, they could remove every single admitted patient out of your ED within an hour of admission order-processing. How? Where would the patients go? To exactly the same spots they go in the ED: hallways, closets, or doubled up in rooms.

Suggest this to senior administrators and they'll spit out their coffee, As ED leaders, you must be ready to offer a quick explanation.

Dr. Peter Vicchellio developed this approach at Stony Brook University Hospital, New York.[39] Using his ideas, the concept may be explained as follows. Imagine a hospital with 10 wards that are all full. All the wards are "over capacity" at 105%; they already have more patients than the number of nursing care spaces available. That is, nurses have more patients assigned to them than they otherwise would, say, 6.25 patients per nurse instead of the usual 6:1 ratio. Now imagine that one of the 10 wards represents the emergency department. Pretend the ED sits at only 150% capacity, much less crowded than at peak times. Now consider:

1 Of the 10 wards in this overcrowded hospital, what would be the safest location to put the next admitted patient?

2 Should the next patient go to one of the wards that are at 105% capacity, or should they go to a ward that is at 150% capacity?

3 Or, to put it another way, if you have one lifeboat holding two passengers more than ideal, and another boat with eight passengers more than ideal, where is the safer spot to put the next passenger?

Hospital administrators hate discussing the Full Capacity Protocol, because they cannot argue against it. Without question, it is much safer to spread patients out across the hospital than to continue overloading one ward far beyond reason.

So why do hospitals do it? Why do they choose to overcrowd emergency departments?

Because that hurts the least. Administrators would rather put up with a few outbursts from the ED than listen to outbursts from all 10 wards. What's more, they figure that the emergency department will eventually tire of complaining, or become embarrassed at being perceived as whiners. Strangely, in the same way that seasoned emergency providers risk becoming immune to patient suffering, administrators become impervious to repeated complaints from that clinical area. They start to see *you* as a problem.

Vicchellio's Full Capacity Protocol empties the ED and improves efficiency and flow in the whole hospital. When wards know they can expect an extra patient at 1000 and 1400, regardless of how many patients they already have, patient flow increases. Magically, patients never wait more than a few hours in a hallway. But if left in the ED, patients wait 30 hours for a bed in Ontario; they will spend 30 hours on a hard stretcher, in a busy ED, with continuous noise and bright lights, no shower, no privacy, when they are acutely ill. Would you want that for someone in your family? In a personal conversation Dr. Viccellio told me he also advises hospitals to smooth elective admissions throughout the week, complete all in-patient discharges before noon, increase discharges on weekends, and try to move the hospital to a six- or seven-day/week institution to improve patient flow.

Don't bother mentioning this to your hospital's senior team more than once or twice or they'll start cringing when they see you walking down the hallway. This advice almost needs to be mandated from the state, in Canada's current model, where admitted patients are seen as cost centres, not revenue generators.

Adrift in a Governance Mush

Hospital leaders do not have clear authority to operate as they think best. They don't have one line of responsibility to shareholders or the board. They have to kowtow to many parties: unions, physicians, regional health authorities, the Ministry of Health in their province, and politicians.

Leaders have been handed a governance mush, and they deliver mushy results. It becomes almost impossible to create fundamental change when so many people have a say in the direction of a hospital. CEOs function more like a UN representative than like the leader of a business.

Hospital boards have the same shipload of stakeholders to please, all of whom have different desires. Boards settle for trying not to stand out, trying not to change things too much. It takes a very special group of hospital leaders to make meaningful change to patient flow in our current system. (We will return to this in step #10, "Get Political.")

STEP# **8**

Expect Resistance and Prepare for It

H AVING read this far, you now have the practical tips and advice you need to revamp ED patient flow. But that is not enough. Step #8 and the next two steps give you a taste of problems, battles, and issues that we had to address at Southlake Regional and St. Joseph's. These steps do not form a comprehensive approach to change management. Instead they highlight some of the issues and ideas that presented particular challenges for our team and share some favourite solutions.

Step #8 starts by looking at staff concerns about change as they relate to nurses and doctors, then moves on to issues that apply primarily to doctors. It ends by looking at challenges raised by change and describes how you can counter "sound bites" – popular admin-speak – designed to stymy system change.

Staff Concerns About Change

Two principles undergird this section of step #8:

1 Treat everyone the same as your most privileged patients.

2 Staff your department like a restaurant, based on customer demand.

The changes required to transform an ED as described by this book take time to get used to. Staff members either really enjoy the new approach, or they transfer out. Even those who welcome the changes will still need help wrestling with a number of issues.

MDs and RNs: A Two-Horse Chariot

Steering a team of two horses requires muscle and patience, but most importantly, the horses must pull together. Some horses spend more energy kicking each other or pulling in different directions than they do pulling their load forward.

So it is with nurses and doctors: whether it is sidekicks, back stabs, or not pitching in to help with a surge of patients – such actions guarantee poor patient care and inefficient work.

RN staffing and MD staffing need to be matched as closely as possible. Nurses find it stressful to look after crowds of sick people without adequate physician resources. In the same way, physicians go nuts when RN sick calls, vacations, or maternity leaves create a nursing shortage. Physicians and nurses need to work well together. As a team, they need to pull in same direction, burning the same number of calories for patient care in the department.

Leaders must continually refocus the entire department on the same vision: patient benefit. *"What's best for patients, all patients?"* needs to be asked over and over. Providers naturally focus on the one patient in front of them. They need reminders to lift their eyes to the hordes who still need their care. Those hordes are their patients, too.

Pulling together, an emergency department is unstoppable. If everyone keeps beating the same drum – *What's best for our patients?* – disharmony within the ED will be resolved and criticisms from other departments won't stick.

Get the Right People on the Bus

The nurse leaders I interviewed said a number of times that if you have the chance, *"hire well."* In *Good to Great*, Jim Collins writes that getting the right people on the bus determined the success of the companies he studied.[40] That makes sense when it comes to EDs. Some people hate change and resist it at every opportunity. These people can make change almost impossible. Cull them out when hiring. Set change expectations early for new staff. Every member plays a critical role.

Note that EDs do not need blind followers. They need everyone committed to the same vision but with the courage to discuss issues with leaders and push back. Any team that quietly acquiesces to a leader is headed for problems.

Some people intrinsically enjoy helping people. Some providers naturally focus on patient needs before their own; they think, talk, and behave in patient-centred ways without having to be reminded. Hire these kinds of people.

When pressured by human resource shortages, leaders tend to hire anyone with a pulse. Don't do it. Employing people who do not really believe in providing great patient service will create years of work for anyone trying to change the culture of a group. In fact, the culture may never change. Once the culture is poisoned, new hires will quickly adapt to it.

Find great staff by interviewing carefully, checking references, and then trying staff out for a few months. Keep them accountable to the promises they made in their interview. Check in frequently. Decide carefully who will stay on the team. It requires enormous effort to select and re-recruit great staff, but doing so makes all the difference between a team that never changes and always underperforms and one that continually improves toward excellence.

Fire When Necessary

Leaders pale at the thought of fighting with employees, unions, and human resource departments to get rid of low-performing staff. It must be done. The team needs to know that leadership supports them by making sure everyone performs equally well. Staff grumble at some layoffs, but they appreciate knowing that leadership takes performance seriously. They grumble even more when leaders don't make hard decisions.

Meet with low performers for performance reviews. Offer concrete ways to improve. After three meetings without meaningful improvement, help them find work elsewhere. I know this seems to create more work and pain than it's worth in our current public hospital system. Enlist the support of human resources experts, legal advisors, public relations, and senior management. Just get it done. Managers hate this part of their job, but the fear of firing will ruin any hope of success more than any other factor. Fire, transfer, or retire staff who cannot be positive and supportive of change. There are plenty of other like-minded teams they can work with elsewhere.

Issues That Apply Specifically to MDs

Physicians have their own reasons to complain about the changes required to transform their ED. The most common ones include:

1 *Irregular shift start times.* Physicians appreciate predictability. Even when they know that flexible start times improve flow, many find it difficult to deal with unpredictability (and their families complain about it, too). It takes many months for doctors to get the hang of anticipating when they most likely will be needed based on who's working each day. With practice, most do get very good at guessing when they will be needed. Flexible shift times become predictably flexible based on individualized work capacity.

2 *Irregular shift end times.* Physicians can leave when they planned to if they really have to get out. However, they often feel responsible and stay to see a few more patients to keep wait times down, or to avoid calling the on-call physician.

3 *Cancellation of shifts.* Again, although this is very rare, some doctors hate getting "called off." Even though this improves efficiency for everyone in the end, it can be hard for doctors to understand in the moment. Some people go to work for more than just an income. On the whole, physicians understand that overall productivity matters far more. Relentlessly preventing idleness improves everyone's efficiency.

4 *Pressure to pay attention to flow in the whole department.* Taking ownership for overall ED function adds a new level of responsibility for physicians. In smaller EDs, a whole department can be assessed with a glance down two hallways. In larger EDs, it is hard to keep touch with overall patient flow. It may feel busy, but wait times are actually short. On the other hand, waits may be short, but volumes very high. Either way, physicians have to maintain continual attention to volumes, wait times, and flow. This adds a new element to physician performance and takes time to master.

5 *Competition, productivity.* Physicians are competitive. When it is busy all the time, slower docs may not stand out as needing extra support. When productivity is watched closely, it becomes obvious that days with "slower" docs on the roster require many more hours of coverage.

6 *Loss of Superman/Saviour-of-the-ED identity.* Super-fast docs lose their rescue role when days are staffed appropriately. Some react to this loss of clout. Others relish their now-acknowledged identity as one of the "fast" guys. Maybe they never realized it before themselves. In an appropriately scheduled department, they see their true productivity by how many shifts are staffed around them.

7 *Transparency of productivity.* Physicians believe anyone who delivers care in less time than they do must be cutting corners

and providing low-quality care. Deep down, many physicians believe *"the highest-quality care happens at precisely the speed at which I provide it, or could provide it, if I chose to work at my top speed."* Of course, this is nonsense. Great departments find value in the unique style of each MD's work. Clinical speed cannot be ignored when productivity is under close scrutiny.

8 *Loss of control.* Depending on the scheduling system teams are used to, changing an ED to a system that relies on a scheduler matching productivity with hours of coverage requires MDs to develop a level of trust many of them cannot stand. They feel that too much power is being given to the scheduler. Having said that, the scheduler is only as good as the results delivered. Even with great results, however, many doctors find it especially challenging to trust schedulers.

A Team of Independent Thinkers

Emergency physicians make decisions quickly, often by themselves and with insufficient information. They get criticized as being cowboys, but you have to be a bit of one to survive the front lines of emergency care. Many leaders, especially ones who have not worked clinically in the ED, do not understand how fundamentally different emergency physicians are from other doctors. My retelling of a parable that's made the rounds in medical circles might help.

Three physicians went hunting: a pathologist, a surgeon, and an emergency physician. As they snuck along under the maple branches at the edge of a pasture, the pathologist froze.

"What?" the surgeon whispered.

Barely moving, the pathologist lifted his index finger toward the horizon. The surgeon and emerg doc wrinkled their noses, frowned, and squinted at the pathologist's imaginary prey.

Articulating his sniper rifle onto the motion-dampening

tripod, the pathologist fired off a single, low-calibre, hollow-tip, high-velocity round at his prey, 1500 meters away.

"I severed the pons just above the dens. Instant kill," he said.

The other two slowly bobbed their heads, raised their eyebrows, and made low whistling sounds as they headed off toward the kill nearly two kilometers away.

"I get the next one," the surgeon said, grumpy that the pathologist had fired first.

Seconds later, the team spotted something a few hundred yards out. As the emerg doc and pathologist discussed whether the animal was in season, a cannon blast severed their conversation.

"Had to be done. No sense messing around," the surgeon said in defence of the giant gun he had just fired. "That groundhog didn't feel a thing."

The pathologist rolled his eyes and smirked, while the emerg doc stirred the air quickly with his index finger in circles around his ear. "Crazy!" he mouthed, raising his eyebrows.

Fearing they had scared off any living thing for miles, the three kept walking. Every crunch of dry leaves seemed amplified in the still afternoon until...

A rustle overhead...

Pow! Ka-boom-boom-boom! Ka-chow! Bam, bam, BAM! The emerg doc emptied the magazine of his shotgun, his rifle, and sidearm before the other two could even look up.

Leaves and branches floated down from the trees through the gun smoke.

The emerg doc, wide-eyed, turned and said, "What the heck was that?"

Emergencies make physicians very independent. They get used to making quick decisions with limited information to save lives. While that makes them great for trauma, it can also make them difficult to lead. This characteristic alone can make relationships with senior hospital leaders almost impossible.

So, instead of "leading" emerg docs, let each of them lead something on their own. Give leadership responsibility to every single physician member; let them each take ownership for a tiny part of the department. Whether it's coordinating students, reviewing protocols, standing in to attend the medical advisory committee, buying gifts for the nurses, taking care of special equipment (e.g., U/S machine), helping with IT, or researching mobile phones, the department benefits when all physicians contribute and see for themselves how tough it is to lead.

Canadian hospitals hire physician leaders part time, which means they'll never be able to do all the work required to run a department well. Getting all of the physicians to contribute increases their sense of ownership, unifies the department's vision, and presents a united voice to other caregivers and administration.

Teamwork

Dozens of books teach teamwork but miss the important issue of the innate subversiveness of teams. If they are not subversive, they serve only secondary needs. Teams must have the organizational strength and sophistication to challenge power. The best teams function as autonomous institutions that align their interests with those of the larger organization in which they function.

This terrifies weak senior management. Strong leaders celebrate it; they care more about great outcomes than protecting their fief. Weak leaders care most about control and pleasing their superiors.

The members of the team need to gain part of their identity from the team itself. The team itself, meanwhile, needs to get some of its character from the individuals on it.

This thinking goes against the individualistic thinking

often required to provide high-quality acute care. No question, radical individualism – the lone cowboy – creates big problems in acute care. At the same time, clinicians who cannot function as confident individualists in the face of acute, critical need end up harming patients. Patient need often demands that clinicians act at the same time they call staff for help.

Physicians, especially, should understand and welcome the benefits of group membership. They should see practical value that rewards contribution and offers support for everything from backup, shift coverage, trades, and expert opinion to legal advice, coaching, and social input.

Too often, physicians see the hospital primarily as a means to support their work. Physicians tend to distance themselves from owning department outcomes when those outcomes fall below expectations. This drives them to see themselves as responsible for managing their own shift, the tiny corner of the organization they can impact. In many cases, this mirrors their binary attitude toward government or other large organizations: that there are only individuals and the leviathan. This thinking, while understandable, will never create a top-performing department.

Finally, leaders often promote teamwork as a means to drive efficiency or other operational outcomes that leaders value. Staff members see though this. Teams must benefit team members first. Operational benefits will follow. Senior leaders who are threatened by strong teams below them probably shouldn't be in leadership.

Challenges Raised by Change
Change-Averse?

By nature, clinicians cling to what seems to work. Even with proof that things are not working well, they still prefer what is familiar. For most, innovation is attractive only when it comes with stacks of supporting evidence.

Emergency physicians and nurses are a bit contradictory in their nature.

On the one hand, they learn to make confident decisions and act in the face of imminent death. They spring into action when those around them are frozen with indecision. If trauma team leaders were asked to form a committee to agree on the million little decisions made for one trauma patient, no care would proceed. Trauma physicians decide because they have to. They move forward, or patients die. They act on less than perfect or complete information and do what seems best in the moment.

On the other hand, they have a terrible time learning from minute-to-minute changes and adjusting on-the-fly when it comes to process improvement. They want to know every single detail up front. They want to have all the decisions considered and contingencies accounted for far ahead of time. They need certainty before moving ahead.

Modern process-improvement methods use rapid cycles of plan-do-study-act. Complex processes don't allow for complete maps of how innovation will work. Things need to be tried and adjusted based on how situations change, in exactly the same way clinicians try and then adjust their approach based on how acutely ill patients respond to therapy.

Be Forthcoming

Winston Churchill's "We will fight them..." speech roused England to resist the Nazi army. It rallied citizens to march, fly, and sail to their death. They fought. Did Churchill have all the details of how the war would progress ahead of time? Did he know when *he* might give up? Was he a "victory or death" kind of guy? Might he have thrown in the towel at some point? Did he have plans he never shared with the troops?

Churchill was aware he could never know how to approach

every moment of the war. Instead, he got the best people in place and led them through a myriad of impossible decisions.

If World War II were an emergency department, many clinicians would never have accepted that approach. They would have wanted to know *how* we were going to fight them, on *which* beaches and *which* airstrips. They would have wanted to know all the details of backup plans. They would have wanted to know that they would have full control over how each decision was being made.

The point is not to say how much our ED is like a war zone or how our leaders are like Churchill. The point is that Churchill had no idea of all the details of the war when he led the country into it. He just went. Leaders need to act on incomplete facts and partially formed plans. They need to adjust to feedback as the team learns. Followers need to support them in it. Churchill did not share all the details not because he was hiding them but because he didn't have them.

Develop an Ear for Complaints

Most administrators care most about promotion and not losing their job. Like politicians, they are keenly sensitive to constituents' complaints. They tolerate only minor, low-level complaining. Major complaints – allegations of bullying and disrespect and accusations of not engaging – dissolve them into warm jelly.

As Richard Farson explains in his book *Management of the Absurd*, paradoxically, the more things are improved for staff, the more they will complain.[41] But their complaints change. Leaders need to pay close attention to meta-complaints, i.e., second-order or higher-nature complaints. When staff complain about unsafe care or unethical behaviour, leaders must act promptly. Eventually, however, staff will run out of complaints about these concerns. Ideally, their complaints will progress to the pinnacle of Maslow's hierarchy of needs:

self-actualization. Leaders can take it as a sign that they've arrived when they hear complaints that staff feel they cannot function to the full extent of their capability and training, or that processes are undermining the expression of their professional ethos. Meta-complaints about self-actualization should sound like music to their ears. These complaints indicate that deficiencies have been addressed and the department has energy left over for higher-order concerns.

Achieve Buy-In

At this point leaders reach the level of buy-in, as described in John P. Kotter's brilliant little book of the same name.[42] Read it. It gives leaders more help dealing with change than days of coursework. Kotter suggests that there are four main attacks against change:

1 Fearmongering.

2 Death by delay.

3 Confusion.

4 Ridicule/character assassination.

He proposes the following responses by leaders:

1 Invite attacks.

2 Respond with clear, simple common sense.

3 Respect always; never fight.

4 Focus on the audience.

5 Prepare for attacks.

Change cannot be stopped. *Leadership is change.* Time changes things even if leaders will not. Patients benefit from disruptive innovations; your whole team will proudly wear the scars they earned through it.

Ever Heard Any of These Complaints About Change?

Well-executed change with readiness checklists, engagement sessions, and all the latest change management tricks will still invite complaint. Here are a few we encountered:

1 You're moving too fast.

2 You're moving too slow.

3 What's taking you so long to get moving?

4 I wasn't at the meeting.

5 I wasn't invited to the meeting.

6 You had the meeting without me!

7 You have too many meetings.

8 I'm tired of going to so many meetings.

9 No one asked for my opinion.

10 You already asked for my opinion.

11 You should talk with those of us who do the real work.

12 You shouldn't listen to whiners from the front line.

13 You should consult outside experts.

14 We don't need experts telling us how to do our job.

15 You're too idealistic.

16 You've lost your ideals.

17 You can't see the big issues.

18 You can't see the details.

19 Why improve what's already better than most?

20 This place has gone to hell.

21 But look what we stand to lose!

22 You have too many details unanswered.

23 Your proposal is too detailed.

24 It's too complicated.

25 It's too simple.

26 It will never work here.

27 It's never worked anywhere else.

28 It takes too much time.

29 I have nothing to do now.

30 I'm underutilized.

31 It takes too much energy.

32 What are you not telling us?

33 Your emails are too long; you tell us too much.

34 You don't expect us to believe that's why you're doing this, do you?

35 Your data are biased/skewed.

36 You collect the wrong data.

37 Your data are anecdotal.

38 Let me tell you a story I heard...

39 You should work more clinically; you spend all your time in the office.

40 You work too much clinically; you should spend more time in the office.

41 This seems to be all about special treatment for x providers.

42 What's wrong with special treatment for y providers?

43 Why should we treat patients as family?

44 Just because I get special treatment for my family doesn't mean other patients should get it, too.

45 We might miss one sick patient.

46 These patients aren't sick; they should wait.

47 These patients could all be seen in a walk-in clinic.

48 These patients need a nurse, a full set of vitals, an ECG, and an acute bed STAT.

49 One bad outcome is enough to stay the way we were.

50 It costs too much.

51 This would work if we spent more.

52 You are asking us to do someone else's work.

53 Someone else is stealing my work; I'm going to submit a union grievance.

54 There's no infection control.

55 We don't need to see infectious patients so quickly; they can wait.

56 It's too stuffy.

57 It's too breezy.

58 There's too much paperwork.

59 There's no paper for notes.

60 There's no privacy.

61 I need more people around to feel safe.

62 There are too many people.

63 We need more nurses/doctors/patients/support in the same space.

64 I feel disconnected from other staff.

65 I don't like working shoulder to shoulder with other staff.

66 It feels like you aren't supporting the team.

67 It seems like you only support the x team.

68 You're dividing the x team.

69 I've done this for decades. I don't need to change a thing.

70 Those new guys are out of date.

71 It's the wrong focus.

72 You just want to be famous.

73 Why don't you spend time on what really matters?

74 You are out of touch.

75 You sound like a corporate pawn.

76 All you care about is x metric.

77 You just want to undermine y group of workers.

78 This sounds like what failed last time.

79 Are you saying we aren't working hard enough?

80 You don't know what you're talking about.

81 If you just changed x, you wouldn't need to do this.

82 You know, this will never work.

83 We need to give more power to the people actually doing the work.

84 This is embarrassing.

85 I used to be proud of working here.

86 I wouldn't send my family here; I'd send them to the terrible hospital down the road.

87 Why can't you admit this is a stupid idea?

How to Keep the Vultures Away

As soon as leaders in hospitals start making changes, they attract attention. As leaders, you never see them until you start to improve things: the dozens of people and departments who roam every hospital consuming large chunks of the budget to make sure others do things "right." Even though these police departments ignore the ED's overcrowded waiting room, they will stop your attempts to improve it, if that involves any change to process inside the ED. Just bring the packed waiting room inside to receive care and watch the vultures dive in.

They will point out that EDs must have "proper" infection screens, terminal cleans, or personal protective equipment, including regulation-approved square feet per person. They overlook the fact that packed-out waiting rooms do not meet any of the standards they expect inside the main ED. And that waiting rooms do not have "proper" exits, ambulance offload areas do not offer unimpeded fire escapes, and EDs often hold far more than the number of people allowed for a public space that size. Everyone ignores concerns about infection, security, fire safety, or vulnerable patients in the waiting room, but they have a peculiar interest in maintaining an appearance of high standards inside the ED. Voices outside the hospital show the same duplicity. Advocacy groups for elders and the mentally ill gave up complaining about crowded waiting areas long ago but still hold strong opinions about ideal process inside the ED.

Making many small changes is a strategy that seems to keep the vultures away. If everything always appears chaotic, they won't have one "change" to attack. If they ever decide to swoop in to offer scathing criticism or threaten embargo, simply pass around a sign-up sheet for them to help with process improvement – and watch them fly away.

Sound Bites to Guard Against

As H. L. Mencken said, "For every complex problem there is an answer that is clear, simple, and wrong." Bad thinking requires far more time and effort to correct than good ideas take to share. Simple, catchy sound bites of popular admin-speak become devils that pop into conversations over and over again. They sound smart and pithy. They soak into the fabric of our minds and shape the way we think about process and care.

Following are a few popular bits of nonsense.

"Match Demand with Capacity"

This slogan sounds especially intelligent because it's short and quantitative and appeals to inner idealism. "Match" almost sounds like the key or secret to an impossible problem.

Nonsense.

Emergency departments must see everyone. They function as if they have unlimited capacity. Instead of matching demand with capacity, the ED needs resilience to quickly ramp up flow to match demand.

"Nurse-to-Patient Ratios Promote Great Care"

This one scores because it is true elsewhere in the hospital. It is not true in the ED. Ratios imply averages, but EDs cannot run on averages. Given an average number of patients requiring a predictable amount of care, leaders could assign a specific number of nurses to provide care for a specific number of patients. But emergency departments have days with above-average volumes and above-average acuity. EDs must excel in the extremes, or patients suffer.

A statistician drowned walking across a river with an average depth of two feet. Average does not matter as much as the ability to safely manage extremes.

"The Literature Supports Modern Triage"

True. Parachutes have also been shown to save lives for people who jump out of airplanes. "Modern triage" is a primary nursing assessment for patients forced to wait hours in a packed waiting room. Remove the waiting room, and you remove the need for a primary nursing assessment at "triage." You don't need a parachute if you don't jump out of airplanes.

"Patients Need Stretchers"

Most do not. If they can wait on chairs in the waiting room, they can wait on chairs inside.

"Low-Acuity Patients Block the ED"

This urban myth refuses to die. We discussed it above, but it needs to be mentioned again because otherwise intelligent people still throw it around boardrooms and on radio talk shows. Patients with runny noses take a few seconds to see and send home. They never block up EDs; sick patients do.

"Quality Care Requires Patients to Wait"

Some actually argue that providing quality care inside the department requires patients to wait outside the department. Thus the "quality" rebuttal pops up again such that we have to repackage some of what we said above. Who can argue with quality? Time to treatment equals quality for most emergency care. Giving "high-quality" care to patients inside your department, after they spent hours in the waiting room, by definition guarantees low quality. "Giving high-quality care inside the department" is code for "covering your butt." High-quality, patient-centred care focuses on all the patients in the department, not just the lucky ones who get inside.

STEP #9

Build on Solid Leadership Principles

LIKE step #8, this step highlights some of the leadership concepts we turned to repeatedly at Southlake and St. Joseph's. It offers models, ideas, and challenges that seemed to form themes of their own. It does not attempt to replace the many excellent books on leadership.

Find Out What Motivates People

At the department level, leaders need to figure out, as quickly as possible, what motivates each staff member on their team. In a perfect world, the same things would motivate everyone. Consistent rewards and punishment would manage performance for all. Of course, real people are far more interesting.

After struggling to understand why a particular change was so hard, a mentor on the senior admin team at Southlake shared his thoughts on the different types of motivations that turn up on a team:

1 *Promise of reward.* For some people, bonuses, higher pay, or other rewards will change behaviour.

2 *Fear of punishment.* Some change behaviour to avoid punishment.

3 *Resonance with concepts.* Other staff members need to understand premises, relations, and logic before behaviour changes.

4 *Appeal to morality.* Many people change only if new behaviour can be shown to align with their sense of morality.

5 *Social pressure.* Others behave primarily in line with their social context. For them, culture determines behaviour.

Most of us are motivated by a mix of all of the above. As leaders, we need to understand and speak to each sphere when we interact with staff. We need to speak to everyone's individual motivation without focusing on any particular one. Telling people over and over that they need to follow the rules won't resonate with 80% of the group.

Encourage Teams to Consider Other Systems

Staff can get so bogged down with an intimate knowledge of every detail in the department that they cannot see the fundamental, core features that need to change. Departments often lose sight of why they exist, what they want to achieve, how they make decisions, and what holds them accountable. You can help staff, and yourself, by hearing core ideas that have been applied in another clinical setting, for example, a high-performing out-patient clinic.

Learn the Language of Influence

Physicians, especially, need to learn how to communicate in ways that influence system change. Nurses do, too, but not in the same way. Physicians spend years learning how to make an accurate diagnosis with speed and clarity. They spend decades honing their ability to pronounce treatment. Patients expect this and go to their physicians for the experience. Nurses, too, spend their lives identifying when something is wrong. Great nurses know when patients are sick, even if they do not have a diagnosis.

MDs and nurses need to learn that the clear, logical thinking once prized by modernism often doesn't cut it in complex situations. People today know that the "right" approach isn't always right, and "terrible" outcomes aren't always terrible. We live more complex lives now; life isn't so simple anymore.

Influence is more than giving the right answer. Nurses often state problems bluntly. Physicians often pronounce their "diagnosis and treatment" for the healthcare system. Both groups wonder at the lack of engagement in their audience. At large meetings, ED staff members wonder whether they should ever speak up, having experienced bad reactions to their approach in the past.

Ideas are useless if they do not effect change. If we leaders on the front lines cannot figure out how to apply our diagnosis and treatment so the system improves, we'll just end up wasting time and frustrating others. Influence starts with relationships, shared objectives, respect, and a commitment to work together.

It's not just what we say, but how we say it.

Don't Hide the Pain of Bad News

No matter how thoughtfully leaders deliver bad news, it will hurt. If it doesn't, you probably manipulated your audience's feelings. Telling nurses they have to work harder when a surge of patients hits the ED, because you no longer warehouse the patients in the waiting room, will cause anxiety, stress, and anger, even if the nurses see it as the best for patients.

If leaders blunt nurses' response by sandwiching bad news between layers of attractive news, the bad news will still seep out eventually and flavour the department. Don't do it. Communicate the bad news with as much honesty and openness you can muster, and take the pain it brings. You are much better off experiencing the emotions, and being present to journey through them, than letting things work out on their own after you leave the room. Let bad news sink in. Feel the anxiety build. Deal with it there.

Work at Getting Through to Others

Library shelves strain under stacks of books written about communication. When colleagues respect, trust, and value one another, they will put up with less-than-ideal communication. However, sometimes important messages have to be sent and heard, clearly.

"Sending out messages" and staff communications can feel to leaders a bit like tapping out Morse code, as they hope someone is listening on that channel. Even if people are listening, it can require at least five communications to get a message through. Even after people have received five communications using different media (emails, posters, letters), they still plead ignorance.

This can be frustrating to leaders, who start pushing back with, *"I'm sorry you didn't get the message, but we sent out an email, a form letter, six posters, put an update in the newsletter, left you a voicemail, and sent a follow-up email last week. Which one of those did you miss?"*

No matter how clearly leaders communicate, some staff will never get messages they don't want to hear. It would take away their right to complain: *"But no one told me!"*

Simple, Complicated, and Complex: Use a New Metaphor

Too often, leaders look for *the* solution to our problems. Healthcare fails when good people apply the wrong kind of solutions to healthcare.

Military and machine metaphors dominate health-care thinking (e.g., cog, mesh, direct, follow, limit, leverage, tune, ramp up, etc.). These metaphors shape our solutions. Complexity[43] offers something different. It's useful to differentiate simple, complicated, and complex:

- Simple is like following a recipe to bake a cake: anyone can follow the instructions and get a good result.

- Complicated is like sending a rocket into space: a team of smart people, improving process with each attempt, can figure out the best way to do it.
- Complex is like being in a romantic relationship or raising a child: success in one relationship, or with one child, is no guarantee of success with another.

Never mind simple solutions; in the complex world of healthcare, we need to stop looking for complicated solutions, too. Complexity theorists prefer terminology borrowed from biology rather than from the mechanistic language of engineering, to deal with complex adaptive systems. These systems are non-linear, and have distributed control (central control *slows* a system's ability to react). In complex systems, size of input produces unpredictable effect (small inputs might create huge impacts); in complex systems, there are large numbers of connections between a wide variety of elements.

If complexity theory rings true in healthcare, how can it inform leadership?

Leadership Principles from Complexity Theory [44]

1 *Focus on minimum specifications / good enough.* Do not even try to plan all the details before you start; it's impossible. Get a clear enough sense of the minimum needed, and get started. This goes against many clinicians' desire for precision and planning. Ask everyone for their thoughts on a new patient flow process, then try it for a few hours if possible. Do not aim for perfection before trying. Perfection does not exist.

2 *Find attractors.* Learn which patterns or areas draw out the energy of the system. Consider leadership to be more like attracting a bird to leave your room than rolling a marble down a track. Sometimes staff care more about vital signs than working less. Find out what matters most to staff to attract change. "Complexity suggests that we create small, non-threatening changes that attract people, instead of

implementing large scale change that excites resistance. We work with the attractors."[45]

3 *Get comfortable with uncertainty.* Solutions need to be rapidly adaptable. Leaders must be comfortable with both data and intuition, planning and acting, safety and risk. Remind your team that leadership feels more like managing a trauma case (organized chaos) than following a chemotherapy protocol (cookbook).

4 *Use paradox and tension.* Lead by serving; keep authority without having control; give direction without directives.

5 *Tune to the edge.* Don't be afraid to stray from the centre. Go to the fringes for multiple actions. Let a direction arise. Healthcare loves staying near the average. If you care about improving things for patients, look to far edges of the bell curve for ideas.

6 *Be aware of the shadow system.* Gossip, rumour, informal relationships, hallway conversations. Most leaders in the hospital do not have titles or names on office doors.

7 *Use chunking.* Grow complex systems by connecting simple systems that work well. You do not have to come up with one, grand solution. Every department arrives at a process that resembles others but is unique to its environment and culture. It becomes a patchwork of (hopefully) great ideas.

8 *Mix cooperation and competition.* Don't think either/or.

Complexity theory offers a completely different paradigm for leaders to consider, especially in conflicts.

Deal with Personality Conflicts

Expect senior hospital leaders to dismiss some of the biggest challenges you face as a leader in your ED as "personality conflicts." They use the term as a diagnosis of discord. Carl Jung first wrote about personalities and conflicting opposite types. Since Jung, conflict became the explanation for everything from family breakdown to geopolitical strife. Emanating from Jung's thought, the famous Myers-Briggs Personality Type Indicator test grounds personality in pairs of opposites:

- Extroversion/Introversion
- Sensing/Intuition
- Thinking/Feeling
- Perceiving/Judging

But administrators twist "personality conflict" to explain all persistent conflict between two people. But surely, personality conflict cannot explain so much. Did Churchill and Hitler have a personality conflict? Are personality conflicts holding back world peace?

Of course personality conflicts are a source of conflict in the workplace. But team members also come to loggerheads over values and differences in ideology.

In his book *Death by Meeting* Lencioni tells us to "mine for ideological conflict." He says we need to debate how our ideas differ, or our meetings will be a waste of time.[46]

Wrestling with conflicting ideas and values feels strange to post-modern leaders. Post-moderns put weight on opinion, context, and environment; everyone's opinions are equally valid; you just have to be tolerant and get along.

Change requires relentless grappling with conflicting ideologies to improve patient experience. We must never dismiss ideological conflict as personality conflict.

Understand Governance

Glen Tecker, a governance consultant, has helped over 2,000 companies put words to corporate frustration and find better ways of working.[47] With four books published, his advice comes in dense packets that might be difficult and time-consuming for you to apply to your own organization. However, the following pearls may help. Tecker says people who want to understand why leadership acts the way it does need to understand:

- What is perceived, is.
- Perceptions rest on available information, accurate or not.
- In the absence of information, we assume.
- Behaviour, no matter how crazy, has a logical basis.

People have little understanding of what they need but strong opinions about what they want. So ask. Find out what people want. Communicate how you can use those wants to add value and inform decisions. Focus on outcome; describe success. Often, people find out what they believe is important only when they are asked what they believe.

People engage when things matter to them, make a difference to them, and are enjoyable for them.

Which brings us to the topic of governance, which is what is required to guide members of the team and the team as whole – required to gain value and effect outcomes on the basis of the team's unique composition of strengths and weaknesses and differences in ideology. You need three things for your team or department to function (to avoid *dys*function):

1 Authority.

2 Process.

3 Capacity.

Without these, you will be dysfunctional. For example, to achieve change in your department, you need support from your superiors (authority), an understanding of what needs to change and how (process), and a team to carry it out (capacity).

At some point, leaders have to wrestle with the size of group – how many people – that should be involved in change.

1 Big groups serve representative, political functions: they govern a whole profession.

2 Small groups serve corporate deliverables: they govern an organization as an enterprise.

Big groups discuss and produce information that small groups use to decide. Do not expect a big group to be involved in all your important decisions at the department level. Delegated groups function on the trust given to them by the larger group. A culture of trust requires:

1 Awareness of and clarity on what will equal success.

2 Open access to common information.

3 Confidence in the competence of your partners.

When you finally get around to making decisions, keep in mind that voice differs from vote. The majority must know the concerns and objections of the minority voice. All views need a voice, but not always a vote.

People know great governance even when they don't have words to describe it. Great decisions pass their sniff test. But organizations get into big trouble when governance stinks. Good governance involves oversight and supervision, but not "snoopervision."

- Oversight concerns itself with what and whether we accomplish what we wanted.
- Supervision concerns itself with what and how work is accomplished.
- Snoopervision concerns itself with what, how, and who does what, which leads to "administrivia."

Governance requires clarity of purpose. Consider a curling team. What happens if everyone thinks the stone should land somewhere different? Desired outcomes are impossible without clarity on what we need to do, what's required to do it, and how we will get the job done.

Facing change, your department needs to ask and agree on these questions:

1 What do we want to accomplish?

2 What sort of organization is required?

3 What resources do we need?

Your organization needs to decide whether it will fund a group, an activity, or an outcome.

If you fund groups, you need organizational charts.

If you fund activities, you need series of business lines. You need to know about programs and business lines within the organization.

If you want outcomes, you need clarity on what they are, first. You must have clear, measurable goals, and a definite picture of what you do not like about the current state before you can work at achieving an outcome. Too often, we waste hours discussing how we will organize or reorganize before we know what we hope to accomplish. Form follows function, and function follows purpose. We need to understand our purpose in emergency medicine. Stakeholder needs, wants, and preferences shape what we decide to accomplish but should not block positive change.

We tend to make decisions using information that is easily available to us as opposed to information that is timely, accurate, and relevant. Available information comes from experience, reading, and conversations. Assumptions proliferate on the basis of this kind of information and often become surrogates for truth.

Finally, Tecker suggests that leaders often get into knots trying to decide who should be involved in decisions. David Nadler, in his book *Building Better Boards*, suggests we consider different levels of engagement in decision-making: the group that makes the final decision vs. people involved in the decision vs. individuals consulted vs. people who only get informed vs. members of the organization who are not involved.[48] Leaders do not need every person in the department involved in every decision.

Manage Great Performance

Leaders hire staff based on clinical competence, and we manage it on our teams. We hire staff based on their attitude, but do we manage attitude? If staff steal medications, they get fired. If you bully the staff, you get fired. But, no one gets fired for a bad attitude. You will never lose your job for saying, *"We're going to lose!"*

Clinical competence is necessary but *not* sufficient for outstanding performance. Without a great attitude, your clinical team will never shine. Attitude must be a key measure in performance management, because attitude indicates responsibility and governs outcomes.

Think of it in terms of coaching. At some point, a coach owns the outcome. If coaches put the wrong team on the field, sports fans hold them responsible for the outcome.

Whole books have been written on how to inspire teams to peak performance – how to recruit the best in everyone. But sports teams already know the answer: Wrong attitude? No playing time.

How do you handle this at work? Who decides which team is on the field in hospitals? Who decides who gets to play? Is it even possible to keep certain players off the field? How do we promote the best? How do we keep our best players in the game?

Peak performance requires teams that function with great governance.

STEP#10

Get Political

EVEN when leaders have great processes and the best leadership team, it often feels to them as if the whole environment is working to resist great patient flow. This step shares some of the irritating obstacles to patient care and opportunities to change medicare at a macro level. Again, it does not attempt to be a comprehensive vision for political change.

It's All Politics

If leaders choose to put patients first and relentlessly crush wait times, they must fight, up hill, against every disincentive in the current medicare system. Very few reasons exist for hospitals, administrators, doctors, nurses, or the Ministry of Health to get patients seen and treated promptly. Political pressure finally pushed the Ontario government to spend $100 million annually, since 2008, on patient-flow performance. That portion of the $48 billion spent on healthcare each year was welcome help.

However, aside from being an election issue from time to time, the actual performance of medicare warrants little concern. Pundits care more about patients not paying – never receiving a bill – than they do about how long it takes for the patients to be seen. Patient-focused leaders have a tough job ahead of them if they have any hope of refocusing pundits, and the public, on medicare performance.

Pulling in Different Directions

High-functioning teams pull in the same direction, at the same time. Canadian hospitals work like a sports team with coaches and players who coach and play for different reasons, aimed in different directions.

Imagine a professional hockey team in which some players earn income by scoring goals, and others earn income just for showing up to play for games, even if they don't score. Assume that both groups love hockey.

Imagine the team has separate coaches and budgets for each group. One coach looks after goal-paid players; the other coach looks after game-paid players. The first coach pays players for all goals scored, with a flexible budget. The second coach pays players for time spent on the ice, with a fixed budget.

Which players would:

- Push to score extra goals?
- Hold back from scoring to avoid penalty or injury?
- Take sick days and miss the game completely?

Which coach would:

- Want shorter games?
- Try to save money by limiting his players' duties and time on the ice?

Misaligned incentives create chaos. Just because players wear the same jersey doesn't mean they're a team. Teams that win have aligned incentives and drive toward the same goal.

All healthcare providers and administrators want to help patients. It's why they entered healthcare. But the system makes them pull in different directions. For example:

- Nurses get paid for hours of work.
- Physicians get paid for work accomplished.

- Nurses get paid from the hospital budget.
- Physicians bill the province.
- Nurses negotiate contracts specifying duties, hours of work, benefits, and grievance processes.
- Physicians negotiate contracts specifying billable services.
- Hospitals save money by making the highest-paid medicare workers, doctors, do non-medical tasks.
- Hospitals *spend* money to help more patients.
- Physicians *earn* money to help more patients.

Helping patients should be the only objective that matters in healthcare. Incentives should be aligned toward that one goal. All providers should be rewarded for helping patients and for how well they do so.

Leaders who want to improve performance, with a renewed focus on the best interests of patients, will have to come up with creative, local incentives that overpower the perverse system incentives in place now.

Let Leaders Lead

Everyone knows Canadian medicare cannot continue without significant change. No one debates the need for change. Popular solutions circle back to: create a private/ blended system, pay doctors and nurses less, and limit the services provided.

Popular books spend most of their time on only two issues:

1 Inputs: funding, expenses, and resources poured into the system.

2 Outputs: quality, performance, and results we get out of the system.

Inputs get more attention than outputs, but more sophisticated observers are starting to focus on outputs. A few inside the system are talking about ways to remove waste, by using LEAN, gap analysis, and other methods. But virtually no one talks about control inside the system.

Understand, and Deal with, Unions

Seventy-one percent of public employees belong to a union, versus 17% in the private sector.[49] Unionization rates are over 90% for hospitals in Ontario. Provider unions have grown imperious. Management fears them. Union members dare not cross union policy lines. Unions make providers the centre of healthcare, not patients.

Everyone in healthcare needs to follow three rules:

1 Always do what's best for patients.

2 Always do what's best for providers.

3 Never confuse rule #2 with rule #1

Unions break rule #3. They make provider concerns paramount and push patient concerns into the background.

Union leaders disagree and argue that they care about quality first. Quality requires sufficient staff, they say, with proper training to meet the quality needs of patients. Unions always push for more staff for the amount of work at hand.

But today, everyone must work a little harder and care for more patients. In the past, quiet times were common in emergency departments. Staff could count on getting all or most of their breaks. Now, managers forced to trim budgets keep staffing levels as lean as possible. Staff work harder than they did in the past, to prevent patient waiting, which invites grievance complaints from the unions.

Unionists are taught from the cradle that nurse-to-patient ratios take priority over patients' needs. Carrying this into an overstretched system, providers actually begin to treat patients with disdain. Frustrated and irritable when they consider the sheer bulk of the work in front of them, they take it out on patients. How dare patients come to the ED with problems the unionists deem insignificant?

Unions hate changes to process unless they clearly benefit

union members. Most often, though, changes introduce uncertainty concerning how union members will fare. Thus, unionists posture and look for any reason possible to resist change. They crank up the rhetoric if only to demonstrate their value to the membership. Union politics costs hospitals millions in arming managers to deal with unions, the invisible hospital management. Unionists worked hard for their members to hammer out a good deal based on the status quo. Process change leaves workers exposed, unprotected by the union. Seasoned leaders, meanwhile, make the best of their relationship with powerful unions. They make improvements and changes to the extent that they don't rock union boats.

Discuss Funding After Governance Is Settled

People frame the demise of our bloated healthcare system as an issue of funding vs. spending, or supply vs. demand, but it is neither of these. Whether money comes from taxes collected by the government or "taxes" collected by insurance companies, the issue is not about money.

The debate must shift from how money comes in to who is in control of how money gets spent.

Everyone demands accountability from the system, but no one gives the people inside the system the freedom or authority to truly change outcomes. Too many self-interested, outside stakeholders are working to control the system at the same time. They all think they know what is best for patient care, but very few actually provide care or enable care to be provided.

Authorities make major decisions outside the system and then expect those within the system to operate by them. All the room to lead has been removed. For example, government holds hospitals accountable for quality and efficiency after negotiating a contract with nurses that has zero productivity incentives.

Professionals inside the system need a chance to show what can be done to improve patient access, quality, and service. We might still rescue publicly funded healthcare if we were to look at pockets of innovation where providers are given the chance to structure creative incentives that encourage clinicians to work differently. Accountability cannot be given to people without giving them freedom to control and deliver what's being asked of them. Leaders do not have the freedom to perform if government keeps giving unions, regulators, and bureaucrats more and more power.

Engage and Debate

In the face of dysfunction, leaders must make tough decisions. Too often, we unconsciously choose consensus. We talk and argue. But we rarely hold convictions that require extended engagement. Too often, we think and speak the same as other leaders in similar roles. We long for a quiet life. We seek harmony and peace over rigour and truth. We find conviction bothersome, disruptive. Know this: if you hope to open discussion about perverse incentives, you will invite attack.

Status Quo Survives on Compromised Consensus

These days, people tolerate opinions as long as they sound mainstream. For too long, we have valued peace and quiet over progress and excellence. The desire to engage and debate is thought to be unsociable, even uncouth. We have stopped doing the hard work of engaging in change, of improving our system. Change requires vision and conviction forged on the anvil of debate by leaders in front-line care, middle management, unions, and overall system governance. We need articulate convictions from all angles.

It's no wonder, then, that medicare has remained fundamentally unchanged for 40 years; it's just bigger, more expensive, and more wasteful. The basic structure of medicare is the same, providing first-dollar-coverage for all medical services. Our feeble response to change has been to add more management, more bureaucracy, and more collective bargaining.

Canadian medicare is like a high-frequency television expected to handle modern communication – online movies, video streaming, high-definition TV, cable, PVR – with rabbit ear antennas.

We must relearn how to debate. We need men and women of conviction to tackle healthcare with will and determination. We need to empower leaders to tackle the status quo, all the way from the front lines of emergency care to system design.

The Problem with Salaried Administrators

Most hospital administrators shrivel at the threat of *"union buses pulling up in front of the hospital."* Low staff satisfaction makes them wilt. They work to keep their jobs by pleasing their superiors. Administrators need good news to share with the board, good news to counter the bad news than flows continually from ED complaints. Hospitals give administrators little incentive to tackle the toughest decisions.

This a huge problem. Most administrators are not physicians and spend years working to get promotions into senior leadership from clinical backgrounds, where they earned far less. They fought hard to get their promotions and will do whatever they can to keep their jobs. Their greatest fear is not failure or poor outcomes. Their biggest fear is losing their job. To them, poor outcomes just reflect the challenges of the position: everyone's finding it hard.

Most career administrators aim to be a little better than their peers, and to make their hospital just a little better than other hospitals. They will never seek to radically change process, to be truly innovative. The risks are too high. They would never do anything to jeopardize their salary. Who can blame them?

Putting some "pay at risk" does not help. It just guarantees that mediocre targets are set and attained. Incremental improvements to a sinking ship do not save the crew.

We need deeply aligned, meaningful incentives. In private industry, senior administrators enjoy profit sharing. In a public system, they enjoy "risk sharing": they cannot make more, so they set modest goals to rearrange the deck chairs on the Titanic.

People will never work energetically for a big, exciting goal vs. a defensive, risk-intolerant goal unless they are rewarded for doing so. We at St. Joseph's and Southlake were very fortunate to have worked with a few outstanding, brave administrators who supported change. Those few brave pioneers helped us fight off all the others who resisted innovation.

The Problem with "Clinical" Administrators

Knowledge of the front lines can help leaders govern effectively – depending on the nature of the organization, that is. Walking around the floor of a factory can provide leaders with data on process and workflow. But walking around knowledge workers' workspaces gives leaders little information about flow and efficiency. Sure, leaders can comment on the position of chart racks and computer screens, but the most important processes occur inside the workers' heads. In the case of this kind of organization, being visible and present builds credibility for leaders, but it doesn't improve process expertise.

What about healthcare organizations specifically? A common myth lumps all types of healthcare providers into one big clinical group. Administrators with "clinical" training become experts on process simply because they are "clinical."

Indeed, if we examine healthcare with untrained eyes, it might appear that nurses, respiratory therapists, nurse practitioners, and physicians do basically the same things. They all see patients, travel around the hospital, record findings in charts, and discuss treatment plans. But this is like saying everyone in IT is basically the same: they're all tech people. To the untrained eye, computer scientists, IT repairmen, and website developers basically do the same thing: they work in high tech. Would it make sense if an IT company like Apple had 90% of the senior leadership trained as website developers? Even if they had years of experience, the right vocabulary, and genuine passion for Apple products, would a group of these developers understand decisions about everything that goes into IT? Even if buttressed with the help of consultants for information beyond their expertise, would they have the requisite knowledge and experience to hold nearly *all* the top leadership positions?

Does it not seem a little strange, then, that so many in medicare argue it makes no difference what type of clinicians you have on the senior hospital administration team just as long as they've had experience with direct patient care? People confuse understanding based on external observation with understanding based on actual knowledge and implementation of that knowledge. Having CEOs hang around a nursing station is never going to give them an inside knowledge of nursing. And having them observe emergency physician behaviour is never gong to give them a full understanding of investigation, diagnosis, and disposition. Even front-line providers *themselves* lack an understanding of one another's viewpoints, motivations, and practices. A physician's description of what nurses do and why they do it will be a caricature of a nursing philosophy of care. So, too, with nurses. They can observe physicians their whole career and never really understand what makes them tick.

Unfortunately, it seems almost impossible to remove the imprint of people's clinical training and experience from their approach to hospital leadership. Nurses learn to follow rules and protocols; nurse leaders feel most comfortable with defined rules and processes. Physicians follow principles and approaches. They feel most comfortable approaching issues as unique puzzles to be solved. Surgeons learn principles of surgery, not just a list of procedures.

Training makes a huge difference in how providers think and solve problems, and they carry their specific expertise with them when they move into administration.

The Problem with Non-Medical Administrators

Other than a few CEOs and a smattering of administrators, physicians do not lead hospitals or medicare in general. Most of the MDs in hospital admin positions do not have signing authority, cannot hire and fire, and have no budget.

Patients assume physicians run hospitals. They stare in disbelief when they hear that doctors have a very diminished role in administrative hospital function. If we include all paid leadership positions, non-physicians outnumber physicians by at least 15:1. But physicians bear final responsibility for medical care. Until we figure out how to give other providers final responsibility, physicians should represent at least 30% to 50% of paid, senior leadership positions.

Nurses, technicians, and other allied health providers hold the vast majority of senior leadership positions in hospitals. They are bright, motivated, and personable, and have extra training to help them function as executives. But they do not know medicine the way doctors do. They do not understand the thinking involved.

Senior teams should be balanced with leaders from all backgrounds, with budgets to support them. A token doctor on the administrative medical committee is not enough. One physician cannot provide balance to a room full of nurses running a hospital.

Hospitals in Canada complain about what they spend on physician leadership when it is actually less than 1% of their operating budget. Meanwhile, these hospitals find what they pay nurse leadership reasonable, since they spend 80% of their budget paying nurses for clinical work. Hospitals do not pay for physicians' clinical work and reluctantly fund physician leadership out of their operating budgets.

Forty years ago, medicare bureaucrats assumed leadership and fought physicians for control when necessary. They pushed physicians out of hospital leadership, and, for the most part, the docs left willingly. This must change. We need to train physician leaders and attract them to take leadership positions. Doctors will not apply for leadership roles for a fraction of clinical earnings. Medicare will not run well without physicians holding many of the top positions. I said "many," not "all."

Once we create opportunity, physicians must not abrogate their responsibility to help run the system. Physicians need to value system involvement and not see it as going to the dark side. Without a major or substantial portion of physician members, leadership teams will avoid decisions that might anger medical staff. Only physician leaders know when to push their medical colleagues, despite strong opposition. Nurses and bureaucrats try, but their decisions do not resonate with clinicians and get little support. Physicians do not lead medicare; the myth has to be exposed, and the reality has to change.

From Engagement to Partnership

Instead of funding leadership, medicare resorts to engagement. Engagement is overused. We do not need more engagement; we need more partnership. Medicare leaders want to increase the support they get from their followers; they do not want to give up command and control for partnership.

The same is true of hospital leaders. They talk about engaging people and lack of engagement and otherwise use engagement to explain operational failure and success. Engagement for leaders means interested, positive followers. Interested, negative people are labelled irritants, not engaged. Leaders love engagement, but change requires more.

Peter Block[50] writes that partnership, in contrast to engagement, is characterized by:

- An exchange of purpose
- The right to say no
- Joint accountability
- Absolute honesty
- Refusal to abdicate responsibility

Engagement means support for a predefined purpose. Partnership builds purpose together. Staff engage, but hold back on criticizing leaders in the open, confining themselves to gossip among themselves, whereas partnership demands absolute honesty. Partnership gives others the right to say no. out in the open. It requires vulnerability, humility, and the willingness to give up command and control. "Engaged" followers retain the right to complain about leaders' decisions no matter how engaged they are. True partnership eliminates complaint through accountability. Engagement fizzles when parties walk away, but partnership means parties keep their commitments.

Medicare needs partnership from the highest levels down to the front lines of care. Government needs to embrace partnership, and providers must follow through in all that partnership demands. True partnership would lessen the turmoil of election-driven change. It would allow us to build on success and create meaningful change for patients.

In our chaotic system, clinicians and bureaucrats wrestle for control with talk of quality and accountability. Both sides crave concrete definitions. Accountability zealots want control of providers' performance, as if chaos would reign without policing. Healthcare delivery gets shaped using concrete metrics like HbA1c levels, blood pressure readings, or surgical complication rates. People start to see medicine as nothing but fixing high blood pressure, normalizing sugar levels, or replacing hips. But if that is all medicine is, then it *is* a product that can be managed like any other. If medicine is nothing but matching patients with evidence, then quants can match populations with resources without input from physicians or nurses. Bureaucrats will regulate with impunity as long as we acquiesce to the view that medicine can be reduced to technical outcomes.

What Our Challenge Is Not

Some conscientious ED leaders get tied up in knots worrying about the healthcare system. They worry that medicare doesn't have enough money to provide the care patients need. With EDs being the point of access for many patients, they feel pressured to make up for inefficiencies elsewhere in the hospital by putting costs before patients.

Emergency leaders have done this for decades, and it must stop. Why? Because those who congratulate EDs for saving money cannot be found when we are sued for not providing care. EDs get little to no support when overcrowding causes bad outcomes.

Emergency providers are part of heart-wrenching cases: mothers who die shortly after childbirth, toddlers who choke to death, and kids hit in traffic walking to school. Bad outcomes happen with sick patients. These cases require split-second decisions that lie open to criticism from the armchairs of hindsight.

One bad outcome results in dozens of meetings and external reviews of emergency departments, but no one – not one single person – wants to discuss the egregious overcrowding and unconscionable waits that usually play *the major role* in bad outcomes.

The time for political conscientiousness has passed. Emergency providers are on their own. If governments want to decrease emergency department use, they need to redesign the system so patients are attracted to seek care elsewhere. It is not for us to bear the responsibility of rationing care for the whole system.

What Our Challenge Is

Medicine applies science, but it is much more than applied science. As Pellegrino and Thomasma write:

> [Medicine] is the totality of this unique combination which constitutes the clinical moment and the clinical encounter, without which authentic medicine does not exist. No simplistic neo-Cartesian reduction of medicine to sciences of mind, arithmetically added to science of the body and tied together with a ribbon of moral science, is adequate to explain this synthesis. Nor is this merely biology. Neither plants nor animals – granted they become ill as well as humans – can enter into a relationship with the healer in which the patient participates as subject and object simultaneously.[51]

Certainly we must improve clinical metrics. But meaningful outcomes for patients are often qualitative, subjective, and impossible to measure. How do we measure clinical judgment beyond complication rates? How do we measure communication skills? Reasoning ability? Aptitude in interpreting non-verbal cues? As someone has said, "Not everything we measure matters, and not everything that matters can be measured."

We need to learn how to articulate what medicine is. And it must be hard. It needs to be tough and complicated to capture everything we do for patients. Narrow-minded medicine makes patients secondary. We need a definition of medicine that starts with the clinical encounter and puts patients' interests at the centre. We need tough-minded leaders with diverse backgrounds and training who are committed to putting patients before budgets, politics, and ideology in order to sort out the Canadian chaos in healthcare.

Over to you.

Appendix A

Our Bottom-Line Principles

OUR leadership team came up with a bottom-line list of principles to guide us as we operationalized the 10 steps covered in this book. These principles capture the most critical concepts that underpin the thinking behind the steps. They improve patient flow, quality, and efficiency, not just in the ED but anywhere patients present.

1 Add value for patients first, always, and without compromise. Treat every patient with the same care given to the most privileged patients.

2 Never make patients wait unless it adds value for them.

3 Triage means sorting, not primary nursing assessment (see 1 and 2 above).

4 Time is quality for most care.

5 The ED team is a two-horse chariot: nurses and physicians must pull in the same direction at the same speed.

6 Professionals must do what they do best. RNs do RN work, not clerical work.

7 Unblock and remove bottlenecks.

8 Always design parallel, not sequential, processes.

9 Design for unlimited capacity; you cannot turn people away.

10 Patients need humanity with every encounter, especially when "there's nothing wrong."

Also guiding us were the following understandings.

- Patient benefit should drive everything EDs care about. Rising costs, guidelines, standards, social responsibility, legal concerns...everything else must come after patient interests.
- Great process will take a department only so far, often far less than hoped. Great thinking supports great process and must be in place before building a great ED.
- Outside regulation, by non-ED administrators, governments, or other bureaucrats, can shackle whole departments and make change almost impossible.
- Opinions voiced by other services, no matter how loud or influential they may be, must never be allowed to define how ED leaders manage the department.
- Fear of change can hold a department back. Teams need to be comfortable with risk.
- Great thinking requires great leaders. Choose your staff carefully. Be very selective with senior hires. Promote, transfer, or retire low performers – just get them out of your department. (Yes, even promote them, as long as they leave your department.)
- Unions cost exponentially more for the same quality and service. Some would argue that service is never as good. Unionized employees remain secure knowing they can never be fired for rolling their eyes, pretending not to notice patients trying to get their attention, or being curt, almost rude.
- Incentives need to align across all providers. Incentives must reward desired behaviours.
- Outcomes need clarity. They must be measured and reported frequently.
- Staff own their morale. Leadership can crush it, but staff morale cannot be a leadership performance outcome.
- Change requires support from the highest levels of leadership in the hospital. The senior team must buy in to building a great department.
- Everyone working in emergency care, both leaders and front-line providers, went into it to help patients when they need it most acutely. Other people do not understand emergency care and ED function. Put patients first in every decision. Attack your department with enthusiasm and determination, and share your success with the rest of us so we can improve, too.

Appendix B

112 Flow Ideas

1 Close your waiting room – bring patients straight inside to chairs if no beds open.

2 Use triage to enhance flow: triage = sorting and nothing else.

3 Limit the number of nurses at triage – one nurse can SORT 200 patients per day easily.

4 Have patients self-triage.

5 Use online triage.

6 Use bedside registration.

7 "Quick Reg" – limited registration; just enough to create a chart.

8 Have patients self-register.

9 Offer pre-registration on line.

10 Post live wait times online to smooth patient volumes.

11 Use patient passports – patient education handouts at front door.

12 Educate the community to arrive in "slow" hours (e.g., before 11 a.m. Tuesday–Friday).

13 Educate the community to avoid the surges on Sunday evening/all day Monday.

14 Limit one visitor per patient.

15 Encourage patients to bring med lists with them.

16 Encourage community MDs to send in referral notes.

17 Have on-call MDs.

18 Have flexible start and stop times for MDs.

19 Get MDs to take responsibility for flow in real time.

20 Have on-call RNs.

21 Shorten nursing documentation (1 or 2 pages max).

22 Use combined triage and nursing secondary assessment form.

23 Use physician scribes/navigators.

24 De-zone – move staff to where need is greatest; don't leave a zone overstaffed.

25 Use advanced directives.

26 Use pre-printed orders.

27 Measure and reward MD performance.

28 Measure consultant response times.

29 Insist on in-house consultant coverage for internal medicine, anesthesia, pediatrics...

30 De-unionize – flow will improve.

31 Have nurses do nursing tasks only (carry out orders, give medications), not clerical work.

32 Track RN break times – insist on accountability.

33 Reward RN extra effort (staying late, skipping breaks, going the extra mile).

34 Match RN staffing to patient volumes by hour.

35 Match MD staffing to patient volumes by hour.

36 Never allow MDs to go home if waits are long.

37 Staff extra MD and RN shifts on known high-volume days (Mondays, holidays).

38 Encourage MDs/RNs to work in teams and hand over readily.

39 Stagger RN shift changes.

40 Have dedicated ED X-Ray.

41 Have U/S (and tech) in the ED.

42 Use techs for lab draws and ECGs.

43 Stat labs.

44 Prioritize ED lab and DI.

45 Don't batch.

46 Dedicated porters (RN/tech should porter if porters overwhelmed).

47 Track DI and lab turnaround times.

48 Get a great EDIS (ED information system).

49 Create meaningful alerts on EDIS to identify LOS, reassessments, etc.

50 Have a modern EMR linked to the EDIS.

51 Retire outdated EMRs – an old, slow EMR might be worse than none at all.

52 Consider a real-time locating system (e.g., RFID).

53 Consider EMR on tablets for each MD.

54 Computer terminal in each room.

55 Link ED EMRs with community EHRs.

56 Have forms available online.

57 Bypass ED for STEMI identified by EMS (straight to PCI).

58 Eliminate phone calls for CT, etc.

59 Extend CT hours of operation.

60 Encourage the hospital to work on a 24/7 service model (at least a seven-day service model!).

61 Do not schedule big surgical cases on Monday.

62 Track admits and discharges by time of day and day of week.

63 Eliminate day-to-day variations of admits/discharges.

64 Perform nurse handover on the ward, not by phone from the ED.

65 Get admitted patients straight up to the ward before a bed becomes available.

66 Use a visual bed management system for in-patient flow so admitted patients leave promptly.

67 Use patient flow navigators.

68 Create robust medicine clinic follow-up clinics (next day).

69 Do not allow consultants to "send patients to the ED" and see them there.

70 Teach residents about quality and efficiency as paramount in their education.

71 Use PO instead of IM, and IM instead of IV treatments, if possible.

72 Position EMS offload in front of the main nursing station – not hidden away where patients can languish.

73 Certify psychiatric patients promptly as needed.

74 Do not perform an internal medicine "ward" work-up in the ED.

75 Order all tests and treatments on the first touch.

76 Plan on disposition from the first encounter.

77 Have multi-use rooms (eliminate bottlenecks).

78 Establish procedures to sedate patients in any room.

79 Partner with volunteers – they can help a ton!

80 Establish CDUs on in-patient wards – do consultations there.

81 Give every MD, RT, and consultant a phone to carry.

82 Do not scale down services over holidays when demand always goes up!

83 Encourage same-day out-patient cardiac diagnostics and consultation.

84 Establish direct referrals to cardiology (not internal med, NP, cardiology, etc.).

85 Have everything needed for work in every area (don't make staff walk to the "tube system").

86 Use pre-printed prescriptions.

87 Have the chief call in two or three times per day to monitor flow.

88 Create an internal, real-time ED surge plan.

89 Create a hospital-wide surge plan and link it to the ED surge plan.

90 Give admin on-call authority to move admitted patients out of the ED.

91 Have back-up on-call to support internal medicine consults.

92 Do not allow surgeons to be on-call to the ED on their OR day.

93 Teach all nurses to apply splints and/or casts.

94 Use "just in time" approach to patient movement – don't stockpile patients by loading rooms.

95 Build a Super-Track.

96 Assign patients to areas, not rooms.

97 Use overhead paging liberally – don't walk around looking for patients.

98 Improve patient signage.

99 Use patient instruction sheets.

100 Use a reassessment checklist so MDs aren't called to reassess prematurely.

101 Build a minor treatment area (aka fast track).

102 Get rid of as many stretchers as possible (to limit holding admitted patients).

103 Use exam tables wherever possible.

104 Use some chairs instead of stretchers in the acute area for telemetry patients.

105 Get rid of walls – use curtains to divide most rooms.

106 Eliminate sequential processing.

107 Insist on parallel processing.

108 Look for bottlenecks – be aware of the theory of constraints.

109 Learn queuing theory and how it applies to your department.

110 Learn and love LEAN.

111 Employ an unlimited capacity mindset – don't limit flow for lack of "rooms."

112 Adopt a "get it done *now*" attitude across the organization.

Acknowledgements

In the past, I groaned at acknowledgement pages in books. It seemed to me that authors were just thanking everyone for everything that ever happened in their life. How pathetic. I now know differently. Authors write books the way toddlers dress themselves; we may feel we did it *all by myself*, but we needed lots of help.

Please note: acknowledgement does not imply responsibility, or even agreement. Many people, leaders especially, might go out of their way to avoid association with some of the ideas in this book. I do not blame them. I could not have written the book while holding a hospital leadership position: it might have counteracted the changes we were trying to influence. I offer the following to highlight people who contributed, sometimes by arguing against points in the text. Any errors, omissions, and misjudgments are my own.

This book, and the work it is based on, required the support of an energetic, gracious, and determined team of emergency doctors, nurses, and allied providers. You all know who you are, and I know how magnanimous you were in allowing the leadership team to try new things. You put up with radical change, change that was implemented far less smoothly than I might like to admit. Thank you, thank you, thank you!

I interviewed a group of nurse leaders for their feedback, especially with regard to step #3 on redefining nurse-to-patient ratios. Your insight helped me understand the impact of changes on nurses particularly. Thank you, Dora Feltham,

Donna Hess, Marlene Wheaton-Chaston, and Jill Wideman. In addition, Kim Storey and Kim Nelson mercilessly attacked silly thinking at every turn during leadership meetings. All of you impress me so much. Change cannot happen without truly great nurse managers, coordinators, educators, and administrative leadership.

A group of emergency physicians read through very rough early drafts of the manuscript. Drs. Eddie Chan, Marko Duic, and Guarav Puri offered insightful comments and suggestions. Your leadership at Southlake made change possible. We need another book to tell about all the innovations you have made since I left in the fall of 2014.

Drs. Andrew Siren and Philip Whatley looked over the manuscript and offered help. Dr. Raj Waghmare pointed me toward resources on how to write. He knew I needed them and takes no responsibility for his student's performance. Thank you, Dr. Steve Stokl, for, years ago, encouraging me to keep writing.

Alex Leung, soon to be Dr. Leung, offered input and added over 40 references to an early draft. Alex also wrote and/or edited a number of academic submissions describing these changes. Dr. Darren Larsen read the whole manuscript, wrote a long review, and started promoting the ideas to other clinical scenarios. Thank you, Darren.

The secret of great writing is editing. The secret of a good book is a great editor and publisher. I must thank Dr. William Gairdner for putting me in touch with Don Bastian. Don took a very raw manuscript and turned it into something readable. It took months and more patience than I could have mustered if our places had been reversed. Sometimes I wished he would just write the book himself; it would have been so much better. Don has mastered the art of nurturing an author with grace and humility, insisting on excellence without drowning expression. He must be some kind of genius.

A whole group of senior leaders gave me the chance to serve in leadership. Looking back, I realize that hiring me must have given them a twinge of angina. Even so, they supported, coached, and tolerated my incessant challenges to accepted thinking. Thank you, Gary Ryan, Helena Hutton, Doug Moore, Janis Klein, Dan Carrier, Drs. Nancy Merrow and Steve Beatty, and Dr. Dave Williams. A crowd of department Chiefs and Physician Leaders – too long to list – encouraged, challenged, and offered advice at Medical Advisory Committee meetings and elsewhere. So many of you modelled grace and leadership.

Finally, I owe a great debt to my family. My children, Lara, Kate, Jonathan, and Emma, put up with Dad zoned out in front of a "device" for hours on end. I worry about how I may have scarred your childhood memories. My parents, too, put up with me through long, distracted Blackberry prayer times as I wrestled with this content. Thank you for supporting your son's obsession.

Most importantly, my wife deserves a standing ovation. If "much study is a weariness of the flesh," then your husband talking for years about the same thing must have been mortifying. Thank you, Monica, for your unending support and encouragement, but most of all for saying "I do."

Endnotes

1   Andrew Affleck et al., "Emergency Department Overcrowding
    and Access Block," *CJEM* 15.6 (2013), 359–84 <http://www.ncbi.
    nlm.nih.gov/pubmed/24176460> [accessed 18 November 2015];
    Kenneth Bond et al., "Frequency, Determinants and Impact
    of Overcrowding in Emergency Departments in Canada: A
    National Survey," *Healthcare Quarterly* (Toronto), 10.4 (2007),
    32–40 <http://www.ncbi.nlm.nih.gov/pubmed/18019897>
    [accessed 18 November 2015]; Roberto Forero et al.,
    "Access Block and ED Overcrowding," *Emergency Medicine
    Australasia: EMA* 22.2 (2010), 119–35 <http://dx.doi.org/10.1
    111/j.1742-6723.2010.01270.x>; Anthony Harris and Anurag
    Sharma, "Access Block and Overcrowding in Emergency
    Departments: An Empirical Analysis," *Emergency Medicine
    Journal: EMJ*, 27.7 (2010), 508–11 <http://dx.doi.org/10.1136/
    emj.2009.072546>.

2   John Maa, "The Waits That Matter," *The New England Journal
    of Medicine* 364.24 (2011), 2279–81 <http://dx.doi.org/10.1056/
    NEJMp1101882>.

3   Melissa L. McCarthy, "Overcrowding in Emergency Departments
    and Adverse Outcomes," *BMJ (Clinical Research Ed.)* 342 (2011),
    d2830 <http://www.ncbi.nlm.nih.gov/pubmed/21632664>
    [accessed 18 November 2015].

4   Astrid Guttmann et al., "Association Between Waiting Times and
    Short Term Mortality and Hospital Admission After Departure
    from Emergency Department: Population Based Cohort Study
    from Ontario, Canada," *BMJ (Clinical Research Ed.)* 342 (2011),
    d2983 <http://www.pubmedcentral.nih.gov/articlerender.fcgi?arti
    d=3106148&tool=pmcentrez&rendertype=abstract> [accessed 18
    November 2015].

5 S. Ackroyd-Stolarz et al., "The Association Between a Prolonged Stay in the Emergency Department and Adverse Events in Older Patients Admitted to Hospital: A Retrospective Cohort Study," *BMJ Quality & Safety* 20.7 (2011), 564–69 <http://dx.doi.org/10.1136/bmjqs.2009.034926>.

6 Stephen K. Epstein et al., "Emergency Department Crowding and Risk of Preventable Medical Errors," *Internal and Emergency Medicine* 7.2 (2012), 173–80 <http://dx.doi.org/10.1007/s11739-011-0702-8>; Sion Jo et al., "Emergency Department Crowding Is Associated with 28-Day Mortality in Community-Acquired Pneumonia Patients," *The Journal of Infection* 64.3 (2012), 268–75 <http://dx.doi.org/10.1016/j.jinf.2011.12.007>; Gary C. Geelhoed and Nicholas H. de Klerk, "Emergency Department Overcrowding, Mortality and the 4-Hour Rule in Western Australia," *The Medical Journal of Australia* 196 (2012), 122–26 <http://www.ncbi.nlm.nih.gov/pubmed/22304606> [accessed 18 November 2015]; Adam J. Singer et al., "The Association Between Length of Emergency Department Boarding and Mortality," *Academic Emergency Medicine: Official Journal of the Society for Academic Emergency Medicine* 18.12 (2011), 1324–29 <http://dx.doi.org/10.1111/j.1553-2712.2011.01236.x>.

7 Marion R. Sills et al., "Emergency Department Crowding Is Associated with Decreased Quality of Analgesia Delivery for Children with Pain Related to Acute, Isolated, Long-Bone Fractures," *Academic Emergency Medicine: Official Journal of the Society for Academic Emergency Medicine* 18.12 (2011), 1330–38 <http://dx.doi.org/10.1111/j.1553-2712.2011.01136.x>.

8 Deborah B. Diercks et al., "Prolonged Emergency Department Stays of Non-ST-Segment-Elevation Myocardial Infarction Patients Are Associated with Worse Adherence to the American College of Cardiology/American Heart Association Guidelines for Management and Increased Adverse Events," *Annals of Emergency Medicine*, 50.5 (2007), 489–96 <http://dx.doi.org/10.1016/j.annemergmed.2007.03.033>.

9 Qing Huang et al., "The Impact of Delays to Admission from the Emergency Department on Inpatient Outcomes," *BMC Emergency Medicine* 10 (2010), 16 <http://dx.doi.org/10.1186/1471-227X-10-16>.

10 Steven L. Bernstein et al., "The Effect of Emergency Department
Crowding on Clinically Oriented Outcomes," *Academic
Emergency Medicine: Official Journal of the Society for Academic
Emergency Medicine* 16.1 (2009), 1–10 <http://dx.doi.org/10.11
11/j.1553-2712.2008.00295.x>; Bond et al., "Leading Practices in
Emergency Department Patient Experience" <https://www.oha.
com/KnowledgeCentre/Library/Documents/Leading Practices
in Emergency Department Patient Experience.pdf> [accessed 12
August 2014].

11 Ramesh P. Aacharya, Chris Gastmans, and Yvonne Denier,
"Emergency Department Triage: An Ethical Analysis,"
BMC Emergency Medicine 11.1 (2011), 16 <http://dx.doi.
org/10.1186/1471-227X-11-16>; Gerard FitzGerald et al.,
"Emergency Department Triage Revisited," *Emergency Medicine
Journal: EMJ* 27.2 (2010), 86–92 <http://dx.doi.org/10.1136/
emj.2009.077081>; Sven Oredsson et al., "A Systematic Review
of Triage-Related Interventions to Improve Patient Flow in
Emergency Departments," *Scandinavian Journal of Trauma,
Resuscitation and Emergency Medicine* 19.1 (2011), 43 <http://
dx.doi.org/10.1186/1757-7241-19-43>.

12 S. Agarwal et al., "Potentially Avoidable Emergency Department
Attendance: Interview Study of Patients' Reasons for Attendance,"
Emergency Medicine Journal: EMJ 29.12 (2012), e3 <http://dx.doi.
org/10.1136/emermed-2011-200585>; Maria C. Raven et al.,
"Comparison of Presenting Complaint vs Discharge Diagnosis
for Identifying 'Nonemergency' Emergency Department Visits,"
JAMA 309.11 (2013), 1145–53 <http://dx.doi.org/10.1001/
jama.2013.1948>.

13 CBC News Room, "Brian Sinclair's Death 'Preventable'
but Not Homicide," Says Inquest Report," *CBC News,* 12
December 2014 <http://www.cbc.ca/news/canada/manitoba/
brian-sinclair-s-death-preventable-but-not-homicide-says-
inquest-report-1.2871025>.

14 Kenneth V. Iserson and John C. Moskop, "Triage in Medicine,
Part I: Concept, History, and Types," *Annals of Emergency
Medicine* 49.3 (2007), 275–81 <http://dx.doi.org/10.1016/j.
annemergmed.2006.05.019>; John C. Moskop and Kenneth V.
Iserson, "Triage in Medicine, Part II: Underlying Values and

Principles," *Annals of Emergency Medicine* 49.3 (2007), 282–87 <http://dx.doi.org/10.1016/j.annemergmed.2006.07.012>.

15 C. R. Blagg, "Triage: Napoleon to the Present Day," *Journal of Nephrology* 17.4, 629–32 <http://www.ncbi.nlm.nih.gov/pubmed/15372431> [accessed 18 November 2015].

16 Robert Beveridge, Barbara Clarke, et. al., "CTAS Implementation Guidelines" (Toronto, 2015) <http://caep.ca/resources/ctas/implementation-guidelines> [accessed 17 November 2015].

17 Iserson and Moskop.

18 FitzGerald et al.

19 Theodore C. Chan et al., "Impact of Rapid Entry and Accelerated Care at Triage on Reducing Emergency Department Patient Wait Times, Lengths of Stay, and Rate of Left without Being Seen," *Annals of Emergency Medicine* 46.6 (2005), 491–97 <http://dx.doi.org/10.1016/j.annemergmed.2005.06.013>.

20 Michael E. Porter, "What Is Value in Health Care?" *The New England Journal of Medicine* 363.26 (2010), 2477–81 <http://dx.doi.org/10.1056/NEJMp1011024>.

21 Thom Mayer and Kirk Jensen, *Hardwiring Flow: Systems and Processes for Seamless Patient Care* (Gulf Breeze: FireStarter Publishing, 2009) <http://www.amazon.com/Hardwiring-Flow-Systems-Processes-Seamless/dp/0984079467/ref=pd_sim_b_1?ie=UTF8&refRID=0MDXFVTQDBWY3F11D5NQ>.

22 S. Palmer and D. J. Torgerson, "Economics Notes: Definitions of Efficiency," *BMJ* 318.7191 (1999), 1136–1136 <http://dx.doi.org/10.1136/bmj.318.7191.1136>.

23 William C. Richardson, Donald M. Berwick, et al., *Crossing the Quality Chasm: A New Health System for the 21st Century* (Washington, DC: National Academy of Sciences, 2001).

24 Thom Mayer and Kirk Jensen, *Hardwiring Flow: Systems and Processes for Seamless Patient Care* (Gulf Breeze: FireStarter Publishing, 2009) <http://www.amazon.com/Hardwiring-Flow-Systems-Processes-Seamless/dp/0984079467/ref=pd_sim_b_1?ie=UTF8&refRID=0MDXFVTQDBWY3F11D5NQ>.

25 Jin H. Han et al., "The Effect of Emergency Department Expansion on Emergency Department Overcrowding," *Academic Emergency Medicine: Official Journal of the Society for Academic Emergency Medicine* 14.4 (2007), 338–43 <http://dx.doi.org/10.1197/j.aem.2006.12.005>.

26 Ministry of Health and Long-Term Care Government of Ontario, "Alternate Levels of Care (ALC) Patient Definition" (Government of Ontario, Ministry of Health and Long-Term Care, 2015) <http://www.health.gov.on.ca/en/pro/programs/waittimes/edrs/alc_definition.aspx> [accessed 18 November 2015].

27 Michael J. Schull et al., "Development of a Consensus on Evidence-Based Quality of Care Indicators for Canadian Emergency Departments" (Toronto, 2010) <http://caep.ca/sites/caep.ca/files/caep/files/national_ed_quality_indicators-10mar2010.pdf>.

28 Jesse M. Pines and Judd E. Hollander, "Emergency Department Crowding Is Associated with Poor Care for Patients with Severe Pain," *Annals of Emergency Medicine* 51.1 (2008), 1–5 <http://dx.doi.org/10.1016/j.annemergmed.2007.07.008>; Jesse M. Pines et al., "The Effect of Emergency Department Crowding on Patient Satisfaction for Admitted Patients," *Academic Emergency Medicine: Official Journal of the Society for Academic Emergency Medicine* 15.9 (2008), 825–31 <http://www.ncbi.nlm.nih.gov/pubmed/19244633> [accessed 18 November 2015]; Bond et al; Bernstein et al; Michael J. Schull et al., "Emergency Department Crowding and Thrombolysis Delays in Acute Myocardial Infarction," *Annals of Emergency Medicine* 44.6 (2004), 577–85 <http://dx.doi.org/10.1016/S0196064404005232>; Christopher Fee et al., "Effect of Emergency Department Crowding on Time to Antibiotics in Patients Admitted with Community-Acquired Pneumonia," *Annals of Emergency Medicine* 50.5 (2007), 501–9, 509.e1 <http://dx.doi.org/10.1016/j.annemergmed.2007.08.003>; Judd E. Hollander and Jesse M. Pines, "The Emergency Department Crowding Paradox: The Longer You Stay, the Less Care You Get," *Annals of Emergency Medicine* 50.5 (2007), 497–99 <http://dx.doi.org/10.1016/j.annemergmed.2007.05.002>.

29 Han et al.

30 *The Goal: A Process of Ongoing Improvement, 25th Anniversary Edition* (Great Barrington: North River Press Publishing Company, 2012).

31 CAEP, "Overcrowding – Statement by Canadian Association of Emergency Physicians" <http://caep.ca/advocacy/overcrowding>.

32 Raven et al..

33 Hotel Managers Group Blog, HMG <http://hmghotelsblog.com/2012/08/28/15-ways-to-attract-motivate-more-guests-to-stay-at-your-hotel/>.

34 Thom Mayer and Kirk Jensen, *Hardwiring Flow: Systems and Processes for Seamless Patient Care* (Gulf Breeze: FireStarter Publishing, 2009) <http://www.amazon.com/Hardwiring-Flow-Systems-Processes-Seamless/dp/0984079467/ref=pd_sim_b_1?ie=UTF8&refRID=0MDXFVTQDBWY3F11D5NQ>.

35 James Stodder, Rensselaer Polytechnic Institute at Hartford, "Strategic Voting and Coalitions: Condorcet's Paradox and Ben-Gurion's Tri-lemma," *International Review of Economics Education* 4.2 (2005), 58–72 <https://www.economicsnetwork.ac.uk/iree/v4n2/stodder.htm> [accessed 28 November 2015].

36 "Canada's ERs Missing Mark on Waiting Times, New Statistics Reveal," *The Globe and Mail* <http://www.theglobeandmail.com/news/national/canadas-ers-missing-mark-on-waiting-times-new-statistics-reveal/article16866187/> [accessed 18 November 2015].

37 Bernstein et al.

38 Peter Viccellio, "Hospital Crowding and Flow," 2015 <http://hospitalovercrowding.com/>; Asa Viccellio et al., "The Association Between Transfer of Emergency Department Boarders to Inpatient Hallways and Mortality: A 4-Year Experience," *Annals of Emergency Medicine* 54.4 (2009), 487–91 <http://dx.doi.org/10.1016/j.annemergmed.2009.03.005>.

39 Viccellio.

40 Jim Collins, *Good to Great: Why Some Companies Make the Leap...and Others Don't* (New York: HarperBusiness, 2001).

41 Richard Farson, *Management of the Absurd* (New York: Free Press, 1997).

42 John P. Kotter, *Buy-In: Saving Your Good Idea from Getting Shot Down* (Boston: Harvard Business Review Press, 2010).

43 B. Zimmerman, C. Lindberg, and P. Plsek, *Edgeware: Lessons from Complexity Science for Health Care Leaders* (Irving: VHA, Incorporated, 1998).

44 Zimmerman, Lindberg, and Plsek.

45 Zimmerman, Lindberg, and Plsek, p 11.

46 Patrick Lencioni, *Death by Meeting: A Leadership Fable...About Solving the Most Painful Problem in Business* (Hoboken: Jossey-Bass, 2004).

47 This section is based on notes taken during two lectures delivered by Glen Tecker in Toronto, 2013, 2014.

48 David A. Nadler, Beverly A. Behan, and Mark B. Nadler, *Building Better Boards: A Blueprint for Effective Governance* (San Francisco: Jossey-Bass, 2005).

49 "Unions on Decline in Private Sector," CBC News, The Canadian Press, September 3, 2012 <http://www.cbc.ca/beta/news/canada/unions-on-decline-in-private-sector-1.1150562>.

50 My summary, from Peter Block, *Stewardship: Choosing Service Over Self-Interest*, 2nd ed. (San Francisco: Berrett-Koehler Publishers, 2013).

51 Edmund D. Pellegrino and David C. Thomasma, *A Philosophical Basis of Medical Practice: Toward a Philosophy and Ethic of the Healing Professions* (New York: Oxford University Press, 1995).

Bibliography

Aacharya, Ramesh P., Chris Gastmans, and Yvonne Denier. "Emergency Department Triage: An Ethical Analysis." *BMC Emergency Medicine* 11 (2011), 16 <http://dx.doi.org/10.1186/1471-227X-11-16>.

Ackroyd-Stolarz, S., J. Read Guernsey, N. J. Mackinnon, and G. Kovacs. "The Association Between a Prolonged Stay in the Emergency Department and Adverse Events in Older Patients Admitted to Hospital: A Retrospective Cohort Study." *BMJ Quality & Safety* 20 (2011), 564–69 <http://dx.doi.org/10.1136/bmjqs.2009.034926>.

Affleck, Andrew, Paul Parks, Alan Drummond, Brian H. Rowe, and Howard J. Ovens. "Emergency Department Overcrowding and Access Block." *CJEM* 15 (2013), 359–84 <http://www.ncbi.nlm.nih.gov/pubmed/24176460> [accessed 18 November 2015].

Agarwal, S., J. Banerjee, R. Baker, S. Conroy, R. Hsu, A. Rashid, et al. "Potentially Avoidable Emergency Department Attendance: Interview Study of Patients' Reasons for Attendance." *Emergency Medicine Journal: EMJ* 29 (2012), e3 <http://dx.doi.org/10.1136/emermed-2011-200585>.

Bernstein, Steven L., Dominik Aronsky, Reena Duseja, Stephen Epstein, Dan Handel, Ula Hwang, et al. "The Effect of Emergency Department Crowding on Clinically Oriented Outcomes." *Academic Emergency Medicine: Official Journal of the Society for Academic Emergency Medicine* 16 (2009), 1–10 <http://dx.doi.org/10.1111/j.1553-2712.2008.00295.x>.

Beveridge, Robert, Barbara Clarke, et. al., "CTAS Implementation Guidelines" (Toronto, 2015) <http://caep.ca/resources/ctas/implementation-guidelines> [accessed 17 November 2015].

Blagg, C. R. "Triage: Napoleon to the Present Day." *Journal of Nephrology* 17, 629–32 <http://www.ncbi.nlm.nih.gov/pubmed/15372431> [accessed 18 November 2015].

Block, Peter. *Stewardship: Choosing Service Over Self-Interest*, 2nd ed. San Francisco: Berrett-Koehler Publishers, 2013.

Bond, Kenneth, Maria B. Ospina, Sandra Blitz, Marc Afilalo, Sam G. Campbell, Michael Bullard, et al. "Frequency, Determinants and Impact of Overcrowding in Emergency Departments in Canada: A National Survey." *Healthcare Quarterly (Toronto)* 10 (2007), 32–40 <http://www.ncbi.nlm.nih.gov/pubmed/18019897> [accessed 18 November 2015].

Brown, Jim. *The Imperfect Board Member: Discovering the Seven Disciplines of Governance Excellence*. San Francisco: Jossey-Bass, 2006.

"Canada's ERs Missing Mark on Waiting Times, New Statistics Reveal." *The Globe and Mail* <http://www.theglobeandmail.com/news/national/canadas-ers-missing-mark-on-waiting-times-new-statistics-reveal/article16866187/> [accessed 18 November 2015].

CBC News Room. "Brian Sinclair's Death 'Preventable' but Not Homicide, Says Inquest Report." *CBC News*, 12 December 2014 <http://www.cbc.ca/news/canada/manitoba/brian-sinclair-s-death-preventable-but-not-homicide-says-inquest-report-1.2871025>.

Chan, Theodore C., James P. Killeen, Donna Kelly, and David A. Guss. "Impact of Rapid Entry and Accelerated Care at Triage on Reducing Emergency Department Patient Wait Times, Lengths of Stay, and Rate of Left without Being Seen." *Annals of Emergency Medicine* 46 (2005), 491–97 <http://dx.doi.org/10.1016/j.annemergmed.2005.06.013>.

Collins, Jim. *Good to Great: Why Some Companies Make the Leap... And Others Don't*. New York: HarperBusiness, 2001.

Diercks, Deborah B., Matthew T. Roe, Anita Y. Chen, W. Franklin Peacock, J. Douglas Kirk, Charles V. Pollack, et al. "Prolonged Emergency Department Stays of Non-ST-Segment-Elevation Myocardial Infarction Patients Are Associated with Worse Adherence to the American College of Cardiology/American Heart Association Guidelines for Management and Increased Adverse

Events." *Annals of Emergency Medicine* 50 (2007), 489–96 <http://dx.doi.org/10.1016/j.annemergmed.2007.03.033>.

Epstein, Stephen K., David S. Huckins, Shan W. Liu, Daniel J. Pallin, Ashley F. Sullivan, Robert I. Lipton, et al. "Emergency Department Crowding and Risk of Preventable Medical Errors." *Internal and Emergency Medicine* 7 (2012), 173–80 <http://dx.doi.org/10.1007/s11739-011-0702-8>.

Farson, Richard. *Management of the Absurd*. New York: Free Press, 1997.

Fee, Christopher, Ellen J. Weber, Carley A. Maak, and Peter Bacchetti. "Effect of Emergency Department Crowding on Time to Antibiotics in Patients Admitted with Community-Acquired Pneumonia." *Annals of Emergency Medicine* 50 (2007), 501–9, 509.e1 <http://dx.doi.org/10.1016/j.annemergmed.2007.08.003>.

FitzGerald, Gerard, George A. Jelinek, Deborah Scott, and Marie Frances Gerdtz. "Emergency Department Triage Revisited." *Emergency Medicine Journal: EMJ* 27 (2010), 86–92 <http://dx.doi.org/10.1136/emj.2009.077081>.

Forero, Roberto, Kenneth M. Hillman, Sally McCarthy, Daniel M. Fatovich, Anthony P. Joseph, and Drew B. Richardson. "Access Block and ED Overcrowding." *Emergency Medicine Australasia: EMA* 22 (2010), 119–35 <http://dx.doi.org/10.1111/j.1742-6723.2010.01270.x>.

Geelhoed, Gary C., and Nicholas H. de Klerk. "Emergency Department Overcrowding, Mortality and the 4-Hour Rule in Western Australia." *The Medical Journal of Australia* 196 (2012), 122–26 <http://www.ncbi.nlm.nih.gov/pubmed/22304606> [accessed 18 November 2015].

Government of Ontario, Ministry of Health and Long-Term Care. "Alternate Levels of Care (ALC) Patient Definition" (Government of Ontario, Ministry of Health and Long-Term Care, 2015) <http://www.health.gov.on.ca/en/pro/programs/waittimes/edrs/alc_definition.aspx> [accessed 18 November 2015].

Guttmann, Astrid, Michael J. Schull, Marian J. Vermeulen, and Therese A. Stukel. "Association Between Waiting Times and Short Term Mortality and Hospital Admission After Departure from Emergency Department: Population Based Cohort Study from

Ontario, Canada." *BMJ (Clinical Research Ed.)* 342 (2011), d2983 <http://www.pubmedcentral.nih.gov/articlerender.fcgi?artid=31061 48&tool=pmcentrez&rendertype=abstract> [accessed 18 November 2015].

Han, Jin H., Chuan Zhou, Daniel J. France, Sheng Zhong, Ian Jones, Alan B. Storrow, et al. "The Effect of Emergency Department Expansion on Emergency Department Overcrowding." *Academic Emergency Medicine: Official Journal of the Society for Academic Emergency Medicine* 14 (2007), 338–43 <http://dx.doi.org/10.1197/j. aem.2006.12.005>.

Harris, Anthony, and Anurag Sharma. "Access Block and Overcrowding in Emergency Departments: An Empirical Analysis." *Emergency Medicine Journal: EMJ* 27 (2010), 508–11 <http://dx.doi. org/10.1136/emj.2009.072546>.

Hollander, Judd E., and Jesse M. Pines. "The Emergency Department Crowding Paradox: The Longer You Stay, the Less Care You Get." *Annals of Emergency Medicine* 50 (2007), 497–99 <http://dx.doi. org/10.1016/j.annemergmed.2007.05.002>.

Huang, Qing, Amardeep Thind, Jonathan F. Dreyer, and Gregory S. Zaric. "The Impact of Delays to Admission from the Emergency Department on Inpatient Outcomes." *BMC Emergency Medicine* 10 (2010), 16 <http://dx.doi.org/10.1186/1471-227X-10-16>.

Iserson, Kenneth V., and John C. Moskop. "Triage in Medicine, Part I: Concept, History, and Types." *Annals of Emergency Medicine* 49 (2007), 275–81 <http://dx.doi.org/10.1016/j. annemergmed.2006.05.019>.

Jo, Sion, Kyuseok Kim, Jae Hyuk Lee, Joong Eui Rhee, Yu Jin Kim, Gil Joon Suh, et al. "Emergency Department Crowding Is Associated with 28-Day Mortality in Community-Acquired Pneumonia Patients." *The Journal of Infection* 64 (2012), 268–75 <http://dx.doi. org/10.1016/j.jinf.2011.12.007>.

Kotter, John P. *Buy-In: Saving Your Good Idea from Getting Shot Down*, 1st ed. Boston: Harvard Business Review Press, 2010.

"Leading Practices in Emergency Department Patient Experience." <https://www.oha.com/KnowledgeCentre/Library/Documents/ Leading Practices in Emergency Department Patient Experience. pdf> [accessed 12 August 2014].

Maa, John. "The Waits That Matter." *The New England Journal of Medicine* 364 (2011), 2279–81 <http://dx.doi.org/10.1056/NEJMp1101882>.

Mayer, Thom, and Kirk Jensen. *Hardwiring Flow: Systems and Processes for Seamless Patient Care.* Gulf Breeze: FireStarter Publishing, 2009 <http://www.amazon.com/Hardwiring-Flow-Systems-Processes-Seamless/dp/0984079467/ref=pd_sim_b_1?ie=UTF8&refRID=0MDXFVTQDBWY3F11D5NQ>.

McCarthy, Melissa L. "Overcrowding in Emergency Departments and Adverse Outcomes." *BMJ (Clinical Research Ed.)* 342 (2011), d2830 <http://www.ncbi.nlm.nih.gov/pubmed/21632664> [accessed 18 November 2015].

Moskop, John C., and Kenneth V. Iserson. "Triage in Medicine, Part II: Underlying Values and Principles." *Annals of Emergency Medicine* 49 (2007), 282–87 <http://dx.doi.org/10.1016/j.annemergmed.2006.07.012>.

Nadler, David A., Beverly A. Behan, and Mark B. Nadler. *Building Better Boards: A Blueprint for Effective Governance.* San Francisco: Jossey-Bass, 2005.

Oredsson, Sven, Håkan Jonsson, Jon Rognes, Lars Lind, Katarina E. Göransson, Anna Ehrenberg, et al. "A Systematic Review of Triage-Related Interventions to Improve Patient Flow in Emergency Departments." *Scandinavian Journal of Trauma, Resuscitation and Emergency Medicine* 19 (2011), 43 <http://dx.doi.org/10.1186/1757-7241-19-43>.

Palmer, S., and D. J. Torgerson. "Economics Notes: Definitions of Efficiency." *BMJ* 318 (1999), 1136–1136 <http://dx.doi.org/10.1136/bmj.318.7191.1136>.

Pellegrino, Edmund D., and David C. Thomasma. *A Philosophical Basis of Medical Practice: Toward a Philosophy and Ethic of the Healing Professions.* New York: Oxford University Press, 1995.

Pines, Jesse M., and Judd E. Hollander. "Emergency Department Crowding Is Associated with Poor Care for Patients with Severe Pain." *Annals of Emergency Medicine* 51 (2008), 1–5 <http://dx.doi.org/10.1016/j.annemergmed.2007.07.008>.

Pines, Jesse M., Sanjay Iyer, Maureen Disbot, Judd E. Hollander, Frances S. Shofer, and Elizabeth M. Datner. "The Effect of Emergency Department Crowding on Patient Satisfaction for Admitted Patients." *Academic Emergency Medicine: Official Journal of the Society for Academic Emergency Medicine* 15 (2008), 825–31 <http://www.ncbi.nlm.nih.gov/pubmed/19244633> [accessed 18 November 2015].

Porter, Michael E. "What Is Value in Health Care?" *The New England Journal of Medicine* 363 (2010), 2477–81 <http://dx.doi.org/10.1056/NEJMp1011024>.

Raven, Maria C., Robert A. Lowe, Judith Maselli, and Renee Y. Hsia. "Comparison of Presenting Complaint vs Discharge Diagnosis for Identifying 'Nonemergency' Emergency Department Visits." *JAMA* 309 (2013), 1145–53 <http://dx.doi.org/10.1001/jama.2013.1948>.

Richardson, William C., Donald M. Berwick, et. al. *Crossing the Quality Chasm: A New Health System for the 21st Century.* Washington, DC: National Academy of Sciences, 2001.

Schull, Michael J., Marian Vermeulen, Graham Slaughter, Laurie Morrison, and Paul Daly. "Emergency Department Crowding and Thrombolysis Delays in Acute Myocardial Infarction." *Annals of Emergency Medicine* 44 (2004), 577–85 <http://dx.doi.org/10.1016/S0196064404005232>.

Schull, Michael J., Caroline M. Hatcher, Astrid Guttman, Marian Vermeulen, Brian H. Rowe, Geoffrey M. Anderson, et al. "Development of a Consensus on Evidence-Based Quality of Care Indicators for Canadian Emergency Departments" (Toronto, 2010) <http://caep.ca/sites/caep.ca/files/caep/files/national_ed_quality_indicators-10mar2010.pdf>.

Sills, Marion R., Diane L. Fairclough, Daksha Ranade, Michael S. Mitchell, and Michael G. Kahn. "Emergency Department Crowding Is Associated with Decreased Quality of Analgesia Delivery for Children with Pain Related to Acute, Isolated, Long-Bone Fractures." *Academic Emergency Medicine: Official Journal of the Society for Academic Emergency Medicine* 18 (2011), 1330–38 <http://dx.doi.org/10.1111/j.1553-2712.2011.01136.x>.

Singer, Adam J., Henry C. Thode, Peter Viccellio, and Jesse M. Pines. "The Association Between Length of Emergency Department

Boarding and Mortality." *Academic Emergency Medicine: Official Journal of the Society for Academic Emergency Medicine* 18 (2011), 1324–29 <http://dx.doi.org/10.1111/j.1553-2712.2011.01236.x>.

Stodder, James, Rensselaer Polytechnic Institute at Hartford. "Strategic Voting and Coalitions: Condorcet's Paradox and Ben-Gurion's Tri-lemma." *IREE* <https://www.economicsnetwork. ac.uk/iree/v4n2/stodder.htm> [accessed 28 November 2015].

Viccellio, Asa, Carolyn Santora, Adam J. Singer, Henry C. Thode, and Mark C. Henry. "The Association Between Transfer of Emergency Department Boarders to Inpatient Hallways and Mortality: A 4-Year Experience." *Annals of Emergency Medicine* 54 (2009), 487–91 <http://dx.doi.org/10.1016/j. annemergmed.2009.03.005>.

Viccellio, Peter. "Hospital Crowding and Flow." 2015 <http:// hospitalovercrowding.com/>.

Zimmerman, B., C. Lindberg, and P. Plsek. *Edgeware: Lessons from Complexity Science for Health Care Leaders.* Irving: VHA, Incorporated, 1998.

ABOUT THE AUTHOR

Shawn Whatley, MD, is a seasoned physician leader with experience in emergency medicine and primary care. His passion for challenging accepted thinking and offering solutions started in emergency medicine at Southlake Regional Health Centre in Newmarket, Ontario, Canada. He served there as Interim Medical Director and then Physician Leader of the Emergency Services Program from 2008 to 2014.

Working with a group of outstanding leaders and a motivated staff, he helped transform an average emergency department that had trouble attracting physicians into a province-leading ED. Annual patient visits grew from 73,000 to 100,000 over a few years. Southlake received special recognition from the Ontario Minister of Health in June 2013 for its province-leading improvements to wait times. Today, Southlake cannot accommodate all the staff applying to work there.

To answer queries about the changes at Southlake, Dr. Whatley started blogging about patient flow on a short-lived blog called www.stoppatientwaiting.com. He soon realized that true change required system redesign. This led him to get more involved at the provincial and national levels. He maintains an active blog at www.shawnwhatley.com. He also contributes articles regularly to *The Medical Post* and serves on the *Post*'s Physician Advisory Committee.

Dr. Whatley has served on the board of Southlake Regional Health Centre, on the board of the Ontario Medical Association and more recently on the board of the Canadian Medical Association, as well as on numerous hospital and provincial planning committees. He is a Lecturer for the University of Toronto, Department of Family and Community Medicine, and an Assistant Clinical Professor (Adjunct) in McMaster University's department of Family Medicine.

Dr. Whatley does not speak on behalf of any organization. All the opinions expressed are his own and do not represent the views or opinions of any organization he works with currently or has worked with in the past.

'nformation can be obtained
`Gtesting.com
USA
~10316
~0032B/1047/P